IRWIN GINSBURGH, Ph.D.

First, Man.
Then, Adam!

A SCIENTIFIC INTERPRETATION OF
THE BOOK OF GENESIS

Simon and Schuster   New York

Published by Simon and Schuster
A Gulf+Western Company
Rockefeller Center, 630 Fifth Avenue
New York, New York 10020

Manufactured in the United States of America

1   2   3   4   5   6   7   8   9   10

Library of Congress Cataloging in Publication Data
Ginsburgh, Irwin.
    First, man—then, Adam!

    Includes bibliographical references.
    1. Bible.   O. T.   Genesis—Miscellanea.   2. Bible
and science.   I. Title.
[BS1235.5.G5 1977]   222'.11'06   76-53811
ISBN 0-671-22747-5

CONTENTS

Page

PREFACE 3

1. THE PROBLEM 5

2. LET THERE BE LIGHT 9

3. THE PEOPLE WHO TALKED TO GOD . . . 13

4. THE SOURCE 21

5. THE BIG BANG 25

6. THE MAN-LIKE ANIMAL 35

7. THE BLACK HOLE 43

8. THE BIBLE, TRUTH OR ALLEGORY? . . . 53

9. LIFE BEYOND OUR EARTH 67

10. VISITORS FROM OTHER WORLDS 75

11. PREDICTIONS 83

12. ANSWERS TO READER'S QUESTIONS . . . 87

EPILOGUE 111

GLOSSARY OF TERMS 113

REFERENCES 122

ACKNOWLEDGEMENT

This book, written to share my ideas about creation, was helped and encouraged by many people and was possible because, as Isaac Newton put it, "I stood on the shoulders of giants." I am particularly grateful to Rabbi Lawrence Charney who read the first essay and Rabbi Harold Stern who arranged for my first lecture on the subject. Editorial help came from Mick Herzog and Fred J. Fett. Carl A. Baldasso creatively illustrated my thoughts and Elise Goldberg thoughtfully read what she typed. Also, I appreciate the freedom that my publisher afforded me to "do my thing."

Most important, I would like to thank my wife Mildred who encouraged me to write this book. And, finally, I appreciate the encouragement of my four children and two daughters-in-law, who were the first exposed to my concept, and whose enthusiasm enabled me to complete the book.

PREFACE

The many spaceflights, both unmanned and manned, which have occurred in the past decade, have changed the thinking of a great many scientists with respect to interplanetary and interstellar travel. In view of the reality that such flights are more than fanciful imagination, it is now possible to re-interpret some of the allegorical sections of the Bible and to place them into a credible context.

In this book I have employed various facts from the fields of astronomy and archaeology to verify many of the earlier sections of the Bible [1] (from the "beginning" to Abraham). Previously it had been thought that there was far too little information to verify the earliest sections of the Book of Genesis. However, if the rest of the Bible is factual [5], perhaps the first part may also be equally reliable.

To achieve my goal of verifying earlier parts of the Bible, I introduce the recently developed physical concept of a "Black Hole." This concept is a possible starting point for science's Big Bang theory for the origin of the Universe, and I also believe it to be equivalent to "the deep" which exists at the start of the Book of Genesis (1:2). Then I explain how and why science and the Book of Genesis are both probably describing the same set of events in the evolution of the Universe and of man.

Since the Book of Genesis started some 5,700 years ago, and since archaeology considers that advanced (or modern) civilization appeared some 6,000 years ago, I am able to equate the appearance of modern civilization with the start of the Book of Genesis. This is accomplished by means of one fundamental assumption — namely, that the Garden of Eden was a space ship which carried two "superior" people, and that it crash-landed on the Earth. From this follows plausible answers to some of the most perplexing age-old questions about the Bible.

The history in the Book of Genesis is well known. But there is other information available which is found in what is often referred to as the oral tradition, since it was not written into the Bible. Most of the oral tradition is found in the Jewish commentaries on the Bible, called the Talmud, and in early Church writings. A recent compilation of this material was made by Rabbi Louis Ginzberg and published under the title *"Legends of the Bible"* [2]. Some of this information provides amazing evidence to support my theory. When reference is made to *Legends* within the text, this is the source of the material.

My theory shows that science's version of Creation and the Book of Genesis version of Creation are so similar that they could both be talking about the same set of events. This means that thousands of years ago, the historian who first recorded the Creation in the Book of Genesis, knew at least as much about the details of Creation as modern science. Furthermore, that historian provided a reason for the Creation, whereas modern science does not!

Chapter 1

THE PROBLEM

Archaeologists and historians agree that from Abraham on, the Bible is factual. Enough evidence has been dug up in the Middle East to substantiate much of what is said in the Bible [5]. However, the claim is made that the pre-Abraham section of the Bible is allegorical, and that it is too general and there isn't enough evidence to check its authenticity. But if the majority of the Bible is factual, perhaps the first part is also factual. In this book I will attempt to provide a plausible explanation for the first part of the Bible.

With today's preoccupation with science, everyone, and especially students in school, is exposed to a very strong and steady diet of scientific theory. Unquestionably, science does explain many things about our Universe, and it explains them well. The origin of the Universe is now best explained by the "Big Bang" theory and the development of life is explained by evolution.

However, the first book in the Bible, the Book of Genesis, has another explanation for the Creation of the Universe. According to the Book of Genesis, the entire Universe and all life in it were created by the will of God.

Whenever science's version of Creation is compared with that in the Book of Genesis, the latter is often rated "second best." As a result, there is a tendency to reject the Book of Genesis and, with it, the rest of the Bible as well. This is most unfortunate as the Bible is an excellent source of material for psychology, sociology, and theology. To reject the Bible solely because of its initial chapters is unwarranted.

But is the conflict between science and the Book of Genesis real? Or is there no conflict at all? Is it possible to eliminate the conflict that is thought by many to exist and to provide an explanation which allows for a reasonable "fit"? I believe it is possible.

In this book I will discuss several related fields of science. These include cosmogony (the origin of the universe), cosmology (the history of the universe), the evolution of man and archaeology. These same subjects will then be treated from the point of view of the Book of Genesis. Following that, I will describe a starting point, a point in time and space which both versions can accept. By intermeshing the very latest in scientific concepts with the related evidence found in the Bible's first book, we will find that a remarkable fit exists.

To accomplish this objective, I will make but one major assumption — one concerning the Garden of Eden. This assumption, however, will be amply justified. A final result will be several very interesting and unusual answers to some of the most difficult biblical questions which have plagued mankind for thousands of years. These include:

1) Where were wives obtained for Adam's sons?
2) Why did Adam and his early descendents live more than 900 years?
3) What happened to Enoch?

4) What is the earliest reference to the Messiah?
5) Why was circumcision included in God's covenant with Abraham?
6) Why did the life span of Adam's descendants fall dramatically after Noah?

Chapter 2

LET THERE BE LIGHT

Genesis (1:2 and 3) tells us: "now the earth was unformed and void, and darkness was upon the face of the deep; and the spirit of God hovered over the face of the waters. And God said: 'Let there be light!' And there was light." This is a description of the very beginning of our Universe. Initially the Earth did not exist — it was void and unformed. There was darkness. But what was the deep? And what were the waters? Where were they if the Earth did not exist? Light was the first thing created. Since there was no sun, this light was different from the light we see today from our sun. And so ended the first day of creation.

On the second day, Genesis (1:6) continues: "And God said: 'Let there be a firmament in the midst of the waters, and let it divide the waters from the waters.'" What is a firmament? Again we find the waters — but apparently two kinds of waters. No mention is made that the second day was just as long as the first. Even in our world today, the extent of daylight varies with the season of the year and the location on the Earth. In the polar regions, daylight may last for four months and so does darkness; such a day would be eight months long.

For the third day, Genesis (1:9) continues: "And God said: 'Let the waters under the heaven be gathered together unto one place, and let the dry land appear!'"

A dry land derived from waters appears. Although this is called Earth, is it necessarily the Earth on which we now live? Genesis (1:11) adds: "And God said: 'Let the Earth put forth grass, herb yielding seeds and fruit-trees bearing fruit after its kind.'" We are told that the first type of life created was the plant kingdom. Again, no reference is made to the length of the day.

Genesis, (1:14-16) says of the fourth day: "And God said, 'Let there be light in the firmament of the heaven to divide the day from the night; and let them be for signs, and for seasons, and for days and years; and let them be for light in the firmament of the heaven to give light upon the Earth;' And it was so. And God made the two great lights; the greater light to rule the day, and the lesser light to rule the night; and the stars."

From the above quotations we can conclude that at least part of our solar system was created during the fourth day. Also the length of the day on our Earth was set: this day is just the time needed for the Earth to spin once around its axis. No statement was made equating the length of this Earth day and a day of Creation. Clearly, the use of the word "day" in "day of Creation" refers to a passage of time different from 24 Earth hours. This is also a conventional interpretation of the "day of Creation" in biblical literature. But if a day of Creation refers to a passage of time, how long ago did each day of Creation occur?

Of the fifth day, Genesis (1:20) says, "And God said: 'Let the waters swarm with swarms of living creatures, and let fowl fly above the Earth in the open firmament of heaven.'" Thus, we are told that life starts in the sea and progresses up to flying birds.

Genesis (1:24) says of the sixth day: "And God said: 'Let the Earth bring forth the living creature after its kind, cattle and creeping things, and beast of the Earth after its kind.' And it was so." Genesis (1:26) adds: "And God said: 'Let us make man in our image, after our likeness; and let them have dominion over the fish of the sea, and over the fowl of the air, and over the cattle and over all the Earth, and over every creeping thing that creepeth upon the Earth.'" Now, by the end of the sixth day, the land animals were created and man was the last animal made. All other life is created by nature — "Let the Earth put forth grass. Let the waters swarm with swarms of living creatures. Let the Earth bring forth living creatures." Only man is created by God — "Let us* make man." Man is considered the crowning achievement of creation. Man is also unique because of his rational and speaking ability. Figure 1 is a pictorial representation of the first six days of creation.

Genesis (2:1 and 2) finishes the description of Creation, "And the heaven and the Earth were finished, and all the host of them. And on the seventh day God finished his work which He had made; and He rested on the seventh day from all His work which He had made." The seventh day is a day of rest. The original intent of the sabbath was to commemorate Creation.

---

*The use of the plural term still puzzles biblical scholars.

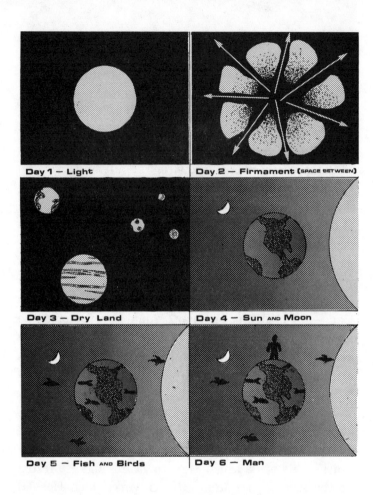

Figure 1. Pictorial representations of the first six days of creation. The first day is represented by an expanding ball of light. The second day shows a division (firmament) between densely packed matter. The third day, the first world. The fourth day, the creation of the sun and moon. The fifth day, fish and fowl. The sixth day, land animals including man.

Chapter 3

THE PEOPLE WHO TALKED TO GOD

The first people introduced in the Book of Genesis are Adam and Eve. They live on our Earth and eventually have children. We tend to think of Adam and Eve as people like ourselves, and as a family with children. Is this a valid assumption? Were they really people like us? How might they have differed? Who were they? Let us look at the available information.

The *Legends* [2] claim that Adam either visited or passed six other worlds before he reached the Earth (see Chapter 8 of this book for more details). In the Book of Genesis we find Adam and Eve living in a Garden of Eden. This garden provided everything necessary to support life for two people. Their food came from the plant kingdom. But there were two trees which were taboo: the so-called Tree of Knowledge and the so-called Tree of Life. The Book of Genesis (3:22) says that the fruits of the latter tree could provide immortality.

Eve breaks the taboo relating to the Tree of Knowledge. She and Adam ate the forbidden fruit from this tree (Genesis 3:6). Because of this, and to keep them from eating of the Tree of Life (Genesis 3:23), both she and Adam are forced to leave the garden where everything was provided, and must support themselves in our world. They have at least three male off-spring who have difficulty living with each other, and the problem reaches a climax when Cain kills Abel (Genesis

4:8). When their two remaining sons, Cain and Seth, marry we are never told where their wives came from. Among later descendants, the biblical record shows that there is a tendency for intermarriage within the group.

Adam and his immediate descendants, listed in Table 1, are very long-lived. The second column in Table 1 shows the life span of Adam and his first twenty-one descendants. Many of the first ten descendants have life spans greater than 900 years. Noah, the tenth in the table, is famous for having survived the biblical flood. After Noah, the life span of his son, Shem, falls dramatically to about 600 years. Then there is a second fall in life span to 438 years for Shem's son Arpachshad. The life span stabilizes for three generations, and then a third fall to about 200 years occurs at the time of Peleg. By the twentieth generation, Abraham, the life span is down to 175 years. Ultimately, man's life expectancy falls to approximately present day lengths.

Let us look at the seventh name in Table 1, Enoch, the father of Methuselah. No life span can be listed for Enoch because the Bible does not record his death. Significantly, there is explicit mention of the death of all the others, but not Enoch. Genesis says (5:23 & 24), "In his 365th year Enoch walked with God and was not of the Earth, for God took him." The *Legends* discuss this further in the section called the "Translation of Enoch." The last paragraph of this section is especially interesting to a twentieth century reader: "To the right of him sparkled flames of fire, to the left of him burnt torches of fire, and on all sides he was engirdled by

TABLE 1.

ADAM'S DESCENDANTS

Name	Life Span (In Years)	Age At Birth Of First Offspring (In Years)	Years After Start Of The Book Of Genesis Family	Years B.C.
Adam	930	130	130	3630
Seth	912	105	235	3525
Enosh	905	90	325	3435
Kenan	910	70	395	3365
Mahalalel	895	65	460	3300
Jared	965	162	622	3138
Enoch	–	65	687	3073
Methuselah	969	187	874	2886
Lamech	777	182	1056	2704
Noah	950	500	1556	2204
Shem	600	100	1656	2104
Arpachshad	438	35	1691	2069
Shelah	433	30	1721	2039
Eber	464	34	1755	2005
Peleg	239	30	1785	1975
Reu	239	32	1817	1943
Serug	230	30	1847	1913
Nahor	148	29	1876	1884
Terah	205	70	1946	1814
Abraham	175	100	2046	1714
Isaac	180	60	2106	1654
Jacob	147	85	2191	1569

storm and whirlwind, hurricane and thundering."

The third column in Table 1 shows each man's age at the birth of his first son. While the first nine (Adam to Lamech) had an heir at an average age of 117 years, the nine after Noah had an heir at an average age of 43 years. Why did the latter group have children at an earlier age? Did they know about the shorter life span? However, Noah was 500 years old when his son, Shem, was born; none of Adam's descendants had an heir so late in life. Shem's birth occurred at a time when Enoch would have been nine hundred years old if he were alive. Was it coincidence that Noah waited until he thought Enoch had lived out his normal life span of some 900 years?

The fourth column indicates the year after the start of biblical history. Abraham lived about 2,000 years after Adam's birth. The fifth column shows the equivalent year B.C.

The *Legends* discuss in detail the fact that the bodies of the first and second generation did not decay at death. Specific mention is made that Abel's body did not decay. Since the second generation is directly descended from Adam and Eve, we can expect this generation to have inherited the physical traits of their parents. However the female spouses of the second generation are never identified, and the bodies of the third generation decay after death. Something must have changed between the second and third generations. In fact, very specific instructions are given for preparing the bodies of the first two generations before they are "buried" in the cave of Machpelah near

Hebron.

According to the Book of Genesis some of the members of Adam's family were the originators of metallurgy, music and the domestication of animals. Genesis (4:20-22) relates: "Jabal was the father of such as dwell in tents and have cattle. His brother's name was Jubal: he was the father of all such as handle the harp and pipe. And . . . Tubal-Cain, the forger of every cutting instrument of brass and iron." Why should the Bible identify the start of some of the major facets of high civilization?

In addition, the Book of Genesis says that members of Adam's family talked to God. It is not clear whether all the later generations were able to talk to God, but certainly Noah, the tenth generation, and Abraham, the twentieth, do have this ability. For God told Noah to build a ship to survive the flood (Genesis 6:14) and also God entered into a covenant with Abraham (Genesis 15:18). The ability to talk to God seems to decrease from this time onward, although Moses is still able to do so much later. There appear to be some final vestiges of this power later in the Bible when the prophets received visions and warnings from God. Today, is extra sensory perception a remaining fragment of this ability to communicate with God?

Adam apparently had some technically advanced and highly sophisticated devices. In addition to the well-known Tree of Knowledge and the immortality-giving Tree of Life, there was a set of God-made clothes that made the wearer invincible and irresistable. The *Legends* claim that Nimrod (Noah's great-grandson) is supposed to have worn them. There is also a very ingenious engraving device, the "Shamir," which reputedly was used to cut stones for Solomon's Temple, but which has since disappeared. The Sword of Methusaleh was reportedly used by Abraham when he and his small band defeated the armies of the five kings.

Even as amazing as these people were, they still had problems living with each other. Ultimately, immorality and evil living led to the destruction of all of Adam's descendants except Noah and his family (Genesis 6:17). In an attempt to improve morality, a Noachide code of seven rules (see the Epilogue) was drawn up to provide guidance so the remaining people could live with each other.

In the twentieth generation, a very formal relationship was established between God and Abraham; specifically, a covenant was drawn up. Apparently, there was no earlier need for such a formal arrangement. As the life span of Adam's descendants was falling and approaching that which we today consider as normal, and as it became increasingly difficult to distinguish Abraham's heirs from the rest of mankind, all the males descended from Abraham were circumcized. Before this covenant, Abraham was known by the name "Abram." As part of God's covenant, his name was changed to "Abraham."

The *Legends* also relate that Abraham was the first of Adam's descendants who aged as he grew older. In addition, Jacob was the first man who declined physically before death. Before his time, death occurred quite rapidly.

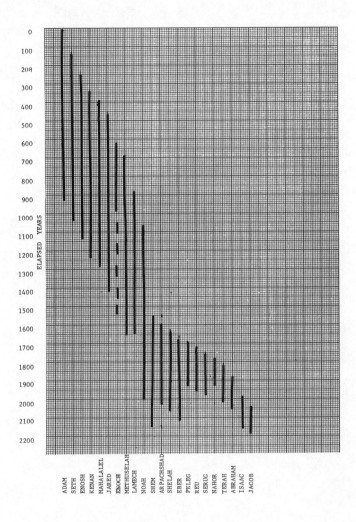

Figure 2.

19

Figure 2 is a graphical representation of the age relationships listed in Table 1. It shows the enormous life span of the first ten descendants, and that many generations were alive at the same time. This, of course, made it possible and quite likely that much information (e.g., science, history) available to the older generations was transmitted verbally to the younger generations. For instance, Adam was still alive when Methusaleh was born and Shem was alive during Abraham's lifetime. Interestingly, the end of Enoch's life on the Earth occurred shortly after Adam's death.

From the preceding it can be seen that, among other things, the Book of Genesis is a carefully documented listing of lineage and descendants. It is the only ancient writing of its kind. It can, in part, be thought of as a family history in which the initial members have some special capabilities which tend to disappear in later generations.

Chapter 4

THE SOURCE

Abraham lived about 1800 B.C., and the section of The Book of Genesis detailing his life must have been written after his death. From an inspection of the fifth column of Table 1, we can see when various events occurred in our time scale. As the exodus of the Israelites from Egypt is supposed to have occurred 400 years after the arrival there of Abraham's great grandson Joseph, the Exodus occurred in the fourteenth century B.C. In the Book of Exodus, God inscribed two stone tablets and instructed Moses to write a set of laws for the Israelites. These laws are supposedly contained in the first five books of the Bible. Therefore we can bracket the time of the writing of the first five books of the Bible as about the 14th or 13th century B.C. The original text has not been preserved; it was probably destroyed at the time of the Babylonian and Assyrian captivities of the Israelites.

The last books of the Old Testament concern events that occurred several centuries before the modern era, and the entire Old Testament must have been completed in the fourth or fifth century B.C. The material in the presently known first five books of the Bible is thought to have been selected from a larger body of material. Some was originally transmitted orally as legends and stories among the early Hebrews. Some of this latter material can be found in other literature, such as the Talmud (the Jewish commentaries on the Bible), and the writings of the early Church fathers, many of which are based on earlier Jewish sources.

It is thought by biblical scholars that the material chosen for inclusion in the Bible was selected and compiled from at least three earlier written works. Ezra is thought to have been one of the chief compilers in the fifth century B.C. There is ample evidence of this compilation. For example, in Genesis (2:4), there seems to be a reference to a second creation when in fact material from a second source is used in the text. Genesis (6:1) is a similar case. At least one of the three written works is thought to date from the period around 1000 to 800 B.C. — several hundred years after the exodus.

The Bible evolved during the first millenium before the modern era. The first translation of the Bible from Hebrew into Greek dates from the second or third century B.C. and is referred to as the Septuagint. This edition of the Bible is the work of some 72 scholars, supposedly six from each of the twelve Hebrew tribes. However, ten tribes were already lost in captivity and only two remained so that all twelve tribes were probably not represented. Tradition says that each scholar translated his version of the Bible, and the present Bible was taken from the 72 similar versions.

The words used in the Book of Genesis represent the best thinking and understanding of its compilers. For instance, their explanation of a modern scientific idea would be obscure to us since they did not have our technical language upon which to draw. If twentieth century technical synonyms are substituted for some of the general words in the Book of Genesis, it becomes possible to understand some of the obscure passages in this fundamental work in terms of modern day science. As we will see in Chapter 8, the use of a more modern equivalent word to improve understanding of the Bible is not a new idea. Maimonides used the substitution of words in his *Guide for the Perplexed* [3] almost a thousand years ago. Some material from the *Legends* can also be understood differently with the use of modern terminology. Together, material from the *Legends* and the Book of Genesis provide the biblical data which form the basis of this present book when the above-mentioned substitutions are made.

Based on biblical data alone, it is possible to count the years since the start of the Book of Genesis. The Hebrew year, obtained in this way, equals the secular year plus 3760 — or 5735 in 1975.

The previous discussion of the origin of the Universe and of man are taken from biblical sources. But there is another version of these events and that is the version developed by modern science. In the next several chapters, I will discuss this version of the creation of man and of the Universe.

Chapter 5

THE BIG BANG

Currently, the theory most widely accepted by physicists which explains the origin of the Universe is called the "Big Bang" — a super explosion which literally blew the galaxies apart at the start of our Universe. In order to understand this concept, let us first examine our place in the Universe.

We live on a small world or planet, the Earth. What do we know about our Earth? Where is it located? How old is it? What do we know about other worlds?

Our Earth is a sphere that bulges slightly at the equator, where it is about 25,000 miles in circumference. To give some idea of the size of our Earth, a man, walking three miles per hour or 25 miles per day, would need about 1,000 days, or three years, to complete his "journey" around the equator.

The Earth is generally thought to be about 5 billion years old. This has been determined from the amount that certain radioactive atoms have decayed in the oldest rocks on Earth, and also from inferences obtained from the study of the lunar rocks brought back by the astronauts. Two thirds of the Earth's surface is ocean water. Scientists believe that life on our Earth originated in the oceans. The Earth is one of the smaller planets in a family of nine planets that circle, or orbit, around our Sun. Figure 3 illustrates some of the details about the planets of our solar system.

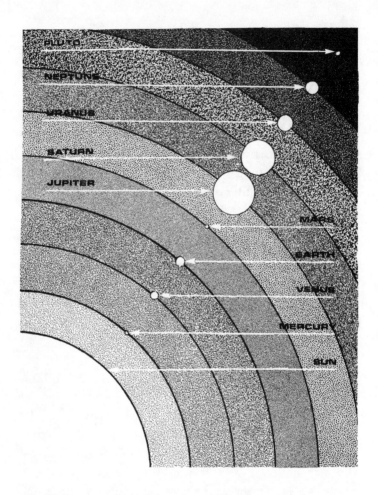

Figure 3. The arrangement of the nine planets in the Solar System. The Earth is the third planet from the sun. The sizes of the planets as illustrated, correspond to the relative diameters of the planets.

The closest planet to the Sun is Mercury, which is smaller than the Earth and extremely hot. The next closest planet, Venus is slightly smaller than the Earth. It is covered with a very thick layer of clouds and is also hot. The Earth is the third planet from the Sun. Mars is fourth, and is smaller than the Earth. Mars has no surface water and is cooler than the Earth, since it is further from the Sun.

The next planet is Jupiter, the largest planet, with about 1/1000 of the mass of the Sun. The surface temperature on Jupiter is colder than that of the Earth and the atmosphere contains gases such as ammonia and methane.

Saturn is the next planet. Smaller than Jupiter, Saturn also has a dozen moons and three thin belts that encircle it. Next is Uranus, which is smaller than Saturn. Neptune is the next planet and is about the same size as Uranus. The last known planet is Pluto. It is quite small but is so far from Earth that very little is known about it.

Each of the planets is under the gravitational control of the most massive body, the Sun. The Sun's gravity holds a planet in an elliptical path as the planet orbits the sun. A year on a planet is the time needed for the planet to complete one orbit around the sun. A day is the time needed for a planet to spin once around on its own axis: for half the day one side of the planet faces the sun, and for the other half of the day it faces away from the sun.

This arrangement, that is, a heavy central body (the sun) controlling smaller orbiting bodies (the planets) at relatively long distances is similar to the modern picture of an atom, which is discussed in Chapter 7. However, the differences in the scale of sizes is enormous. While the planets are controlled by the force of gravity, the atoms are controlled by an electrical force. But the same basic system controls the planets as well as atoms. Although vastly different in size, there is a logical similarity between them.

The sun itself is about 5 billion years old, the same as the Earth and the Moon, since all parts of the Solar System were formed at about the same time. The sun is very large — about 1,000,000 miles in diameter. The surface temperature is about 10,000°C, and the interior is hotter, over 1,000,000°C. The sun is so hot that no solids or liquids exist there, everything has evaporated and only gases exist on the sun. Even the atoms of these gases are partially decomposed or partially ionized.

The sun is a star, but is close enough to us so that it appears very large. Other suns are so far away that they look small and we call them "stars." From the closest star, it takes starlight about four years to reach the Earth, while light from the sun reaches us in eight minutes. Light has the fastest known speed of any type of energy and this gives us a useful measuring tool. We refer to the distance that light travels in one year as one light year, which is equal to about six million million miles. Figure 4 illustrates how distance can be made equivalent to time if the speed of light is used as a multiplier.

There appear to be more than 100 billion suns in the group which contains our sun and such a group is

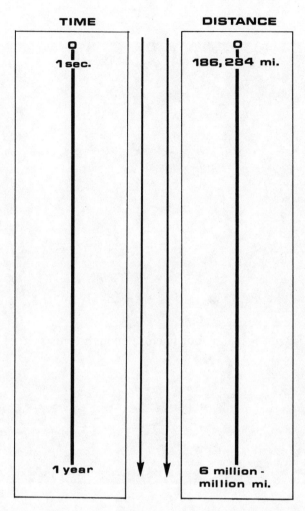

Figure 4. Relationship between distance and the speed of light. Light travels at 186,000 miles per second. Extending this time scale to one year, light will have traveled six million million miles, (that is one light year is six million million miles).

The SUN-
30,000 light years
from center

Figure 5. Spiral Galaxy of type similar to the Milky Way. Our sun would be about 30,000 light years out from the center of the Galaxy.

called a Galaxy. Our Galaxy can be visualized as a flattened disk. However, the stars are not uniformly distributed in the disk, but seem to concentrate in spirals or arms in the disk. Our Galaxy, The Milky Way, is believed by astronomers to look like the sketch in Figure 5. Our Galaxy is about 100,000 light years across, and our sun is 30,000 light years from its center. The sun rotates around the center of the Galaxy once in 230,000,000 years.

Our Galaxy is one of a group of 14 "close together" Galaxies. It includes the two Magellanic Clouds (two small Galaxies visible from the Southern Hemisphere) and also the Andromeda Galaxy which has a shape similar to that of the Milky Way. These Galaxies move together as a group in space. All the other Galaxies and groups of Galaxies, together, constitute what is called our Universe. When we look at these Galaxies, it seems that they all are moving away from each other, and the furthest ones are moving the fastest. By reversing the motion of the galaxies, or extrapolating backwards in time, we can compute that the galaxies started flying apart between 10 and 20 billion years ago.

Science considers the best theory which explains the origin of the Universe to be the "Big Bang" — the super explosion mentioned earlier which literally blew the Galaxies apart at the start of our Universe. The explosion was so powerful that the Galaxies are still flying apart some 10 billion years later (see Figure 6). We know nothing of what existed before this explosion and nothing about its cause. Our Universe started with this enormous explosion. Incidentally, does the Book of

THE BIG BANG:
First light moves outward, with cosmic matter following

Today, pieces of the universe are still moving apart

Figure 6. The super explosion that started our Universe. The matter coming out of the super Black Hole was blown away with such an impact, that it is still flying apart. In the interim, the matter has cooled down and formed Galaxies.

Genesis discuss the Big Bang? We will see on page 54 where the Bible discusses the Big Bang.

Gravity is the dominant long distance force in our Universe. It keeps all the stars in a Galaxy in a group. In addition, it keeps a sun from blowing itself apart, and it also keeps planets in orbit around their sun. It even keeps people on a planet. Although gravity is important, and science has been studying it for centuries, there is still much to be learned about it.

Chapter 6

THE MAN-LIKE ANIMAL

Modern man is a highly sophisticated social being who lives in a structured society and utilizes many mechanical and material things for his needs and comforts. How long has such a being existed on the Earth? What was there before him? How far back can we trace his existence?

After the Big Bang, which was described in the previous chapter as the start of our Universe, the matter in the Universe started to move apart and cool down. Ultimately, the matter in galaxies had cooled sufficiently to form the simplest and lightest atoms in our Universe (mostly hydrogen). Heavier and more complex atoms were subsequently formed in the very hot interiors of stars. Where further cooling could occur, conditions were appropriate for atoms to combine and form simple molecules that are involved in living matter, such as methane (CH_4), ammonia (NH_3), water (H_2O), and hydrogen (H_2).

Under the conditions that existed in the Earth's original ocean, more complex molecules formed from these simple molecules. Among them were the "building blocks," such as nucleic acids and proteins, from which living matter is made. Finally, a simple single celled plant, that used sunlight for energy, was formed. This entire process of slowly developing more complex

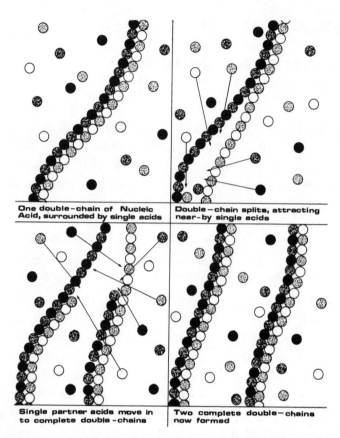

One double-chain of Nucleic Acid, surrounded by single acids

Double-chain splits, attracting near-by single acids

Single partner acids move in to complete double-chains

Two complete double-chains now formed

Figure 7. The secret of life — a living molecule that duplicates itself. The molecule is a strand of pairs of amino acids. Only four amino acids are involved and each amino acid couples with only one other. The double strand starts to split at one end into two single strands, and each newly freed amino acid on each strand attracts the proper mating acid from the available amino acids in the surrounding growth medium. When the entire molecule has undergone this split and mate process, there are two identical copies of the original molecule.

36

structures finally culminated with a structure that could duplicate itself (Figure 7).

The next step in the evolutionary process was a single celled animal that lived off the plants. The single cell is the fundamental unit of animal life, and it can split and form two duplicates of itself. The single celled animal existed in a salty ocean from which it obtained needed chemicals. Larger bodies evolved consisting of many cells with thin films of salt water surrounding each pair of cells: thus each cell is still surrounded by a salt water medium. Additional development resulted in highly specialized cells for skin, muscle and special organs (heart, brain, lungs, etc.). In the human body today, we still find the basic structure of pairs of cells bathed in the equivalent of ocean water, which in our case is blood. Chemically, blood is remarkably similar to ocean water. Incidentally, didn't the Bible say that on the fifth day of Creation, animal life started in the Ocean (page 54)?

The oldest remains of single celled animals are at least a billion years old. Because they did not have hard shells, it was difficult for them to be preserved as fossils in rocks. However, by careful study of the evidence and remains of life which can be found in rocks, a continuing story of biological development and evolution can be traced. Nature tends to favor the development of those animals who can live more efficiently in their environment.

The size of animals slowly increased and specialized structures developed such as fish with bony skeletons and fins for swimming. While fish swim in water, a new type of animal evolved that could "swim" in the air - the birds.

About 400 million years ago, some fish developed lungs. With a modified fin functioning as a kind of leg, these fish came out of the water and were the so-called amphibians which could live both on land and in water. These amphibians, in time, developed a tough protective hide much like our present day alligators and crocodiles, and reproduced by laying eggs, with protective hard coverings.

The reptiles, which evolved about 300 million years ago, bore their young on land. From these reptiles, animals developed whose young grew within the mother's body. These are called mammals and are the final link in the evolutionary chain. Mammals bear very few offspring at any one time, and their young require relatively long periods of rearing because they are complex animals.

Some mammals left the ground and took to the trees, probably for safety. These are the primates whose arms and hands were specialized for climbing. They also developed larger brains and were plant eaters. Sight, rather than smell, was their major sensory organ. Perhaps in search of more food, one of these primates left the trees and returned to the ground. It probably developed more functional hands and a larger brain, and the length of time for rearing the young increased. This animal developed an upright walk and learned to use tools. It became a hunter and flesh eater. Gradually

TABLE 2.

TIME SCALE FOR THE EVOLUTION OF MAN

Years Ago	Life Form	Significant Feature
1-2 Billion	First Life	Simple cells in oceans
425 Million	Fish	Internal skeleton and bony scales
390 Million	Fish	Articulated fin forerunner of a leg
365 Million	Fish Amphibian Birds	Air breathing Live in water or on land "Swim" in the air
280 Million	Reptile	Well protected eggs; laid on land
100 Million	Mammals	Long legs; suckle young; placenta
25 Million	Primates	Grasping hand; sight is major sense
1-2 Million	Man	Larger brain; opposed thumb; walk upright
35,000	Modern Man	Late Stone Age
6,000	Civilized Man	Start of modern civilization

TABLE 3.

DEVELOPMENT OF CIVILIZATION FROM THE STONE AGE TO MODERN MAN

DATE	STAGE	CULTURAL ELEMENTS
1,000,000 BC	LOWER STONE AGE	PEBBLE TOOLS HAND AXES CHOPPERS
500,000 BC		FIRE
200,000 BC	MIDDLE STONE AGE	FLAKE TOOLS
60,000 BC		BURIAL OF DEAD
50,000 BC	UPPER STONE AGE	
25,000 BC		CAVE PAINTINGS SEWING SPEAR THROWERS
8,000 BC		BOWS & ARROWS TRAINED ANIMALS
6,000 BC		FARMING VILLAGES POTTERY WEAVING
3,000 BC	BRONZE AGE	THE ARTS CITIES WRITING NONFERROUS METALS
1,000 BC	IRON AGE	IRON ALPHABETS EMPIRES

it developed most of the physical characteristics of man as we know him today. Table 2 summarizes the evolutionary chain leading to man. Table 3 summarizes the stages leading from the Stone Age to modern civilization.

Thus, the first man-like but uncivilized animal appeared about 1 or 2 million years ago. The most recent specimen, called homosapiens or modern man, made his appearance about 35,000 years ago. But for the next 25,000 years, he was uncivilized and lived as a hunter and food gatherer.

The first signs of civilization appear about 9,000 years ago with some indications of domesticated grain, domesticated animals, and small settlements. *True civilization appeared almost overnight about 6,000 years ago, a date which is very important and which shall be referred to again later.*

The blooming civilization included metallurgy, the arts, animal husbandry, and other highly developed facets of modern civilization. By the way, weren't some of these mentioned in the Book of Genesis (see page 17)?

The two preceding chapters have summarized science's view of the creation of the Universe and of man. On the face of it, this version is quite different from that in the Book of Genesis (chapters 2 - 4). However, if we are to fit the two versions together, we need a common starting point. For that we can use one of science's newest concepts, which is discussed in the next chapter.

Chapter 7

THE BLACK HOLE

The "Black Hole" is a relatively new concept in astrophysics. The idea had been around since the 1920's, but an experimental proof wasn't found in the heavens until 1973.

If we want to leave an astronomical body, we must travel at least as fast as the "escape velocity" (the speed that has to be reached in order for an object to escape the gravitational pull of a planet or other astronomical body). The more massive a body, the stronger this gravitational pull or gravity and, therefore, the higher the velocity which must be attained to escape from the body. As an example, the escape velocity for the Earth is 25,000 miles per hour.

What happens when the astronomical body is so large and the gravity is so strong that the escape velocity exceeds the speed of light? For one thing, Einstein's Theory of Relativity teaches that nothing can go faster than light and therefore nothing can escape from this very large body because the escape velocity exceeds the speed of light. Even light can't escape. And so we are drawn to the concept of a "Black Hole."

In order to understand the "Black Hole" concept we should know something about atoms. A simple introduction to the atom can be made by imagining a few simple experiments. First, let us start with a piece of matter, such as iron, one of the 92 different chemical elements from which our world is made. Now, let us assume that piece of iron is cut in half, so that we now have two pieces of iron. If one of the pieces is then cut in half again, there are now two smaller pieces of iron. Let us keep cutting one resulting piece of iron in half until we get the smallest piece of iron we are able to obtain. This is called an atom of iron. We will know when we have reached the iron atom because when we split it in half, we no longer have two pieces of iron. The halves of the iron atom turn out to be two smaller and lighter atoms, each of which is an atom of aluminum. Each element has its own special atom characterized by a distinctive weight and by a certain number of pieces. Figure 8 shows how the pieces of an iron atom can be rearranged into two atoms of aluminum.

The atom itself has an interesting structure. On a miniature scale it resembles our solar system, that is, the greatest concentration of weight is in the center (nucleus) and there are small, light weight particles (electrons) revolving about this center, but far away from it (analogous to the planets). The center portion of an atom is called the nucleus; it is also the location for the positive electricity in an atom.

Occasionally, the electrical properties of an atom are reversed and the nucleus carries the opposite electrical charge. This is called anti-matter. If an atom of matter is brought near an atom of anti-matter, the opposite charges attract each other and the atoms collide with

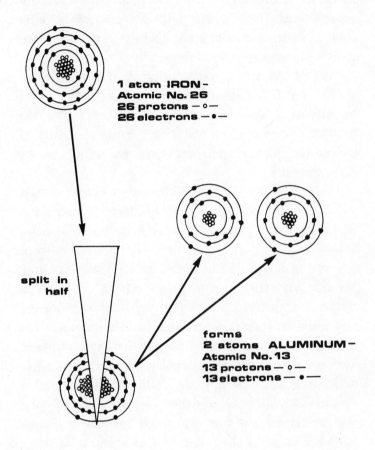

Figure 8. An iron atom has 26 protons in its nucleus and 26 electrons in the surrounding cloud. On being split in half, each nucleus has 13 protons and there are 13 electrons in the surrounding cloud. But this is exactly two atoms of aluminum.

the result that they both are annihilated. Only radiation energy (light, x-rays, radio-waves) remains after such a collision. Fortunately, there is very little anti-matter in our part of the Galaxy.

Gravity on Earth is the pull that the Earth exerts on everything. Scientists are also certain that gravity exists on all other astronomical bodies. Table 4 lists the gravitational strengths and the velocities needed to escape the gravitational pull of all the planets in our solar system.

As a star ages, it gets hotter. It can get so hot, at least 100 million degrees, that all of the electrons in a star's atoms are boiled away and only bare nuclei remain. When the star finally runs out of "fuel" and stops generating energy, the balance between gravity pulling inwards and energy generation pushing outwards is upset, and gravity starts collapsing the star. Since the electrons are gone, contraction continues until the atomic nuclei in the star touch at distances of about 10^{-13} cm. The resultant material is tremendously dense and heavy (a teaspoon weighs millions of tons) and is essentially a huge ball of dense nuclear matter. Such a star would have a very strong gravity. Even though matter is highly compressed in this state, it is not a solid because of the high temperature, and is properly called a fluid — a nuclear fluid.

If the hypothetical star we have been discussing had been at least ten times as massive as our sun, its final collapsed state would be a "Black Hole." In this condition, the gravity would be so strong that the

TABLE 4.

GRAVITY AND ESCAPE VELOCITY FOR OUR SOLAR SYSTEM

Planet	Gravity Force Earth = 1	Escape Velocity In Miles Per Hour
Mercury	.37	9,400
Venus	.86	23,000
Earth	1.0	25,000
Mars	.38	11,200
Jupiter	2.7	136,000
Saturn	1.2	82,500
Uranus	.96	49,200
Neptune	1.53	56,000
Pluto	.81	22,300

escape velocity from such a body would exceed the speed of light. Since nothing can travel faster than the speed of light, nothing can escape from the "Black Hole", not even light. However, it still has an enormous gravity and can pull other bodies toward and into itself. In this respect it is a "hole" in our Universe into which matter can fall. Matter can leave our Universe by entering a Black hole because our Universe can no longer detect this matter. Thus the name "Black Hole" is appropriate. Figure 9 represents the visual impact of a distant Black Hole in our Universe. Figure 10 illustrates the concept that no velocity can escape from a Black Hole.

When a large star dies, it ends up as a massive Black Hole. Our Universe will eventually end up in this manner when all its stars die. In the next chapter, we will see that a Super Black Hole could also be the beginning of our Universe!

There is an interesting way of thinking about a Black Hole. We start by recalling that we live in a three dimensional world. This is the world our senses tell us about, and each of the three dimensions is a distance — up or down, side to side, and front to back. A two dimensional world is that of the insect which lives on the surface of an orange. Since he cannot fly and cannot dig into the orange's surface, his world is of two dimensions — the equivalent of latitude and longitude on the Earth. But Einstein taught about a fourth dimension. It is time-like, and mathematically we can treat it as a distance by multiplying time by the speed

Figure 9. The visual impact of a distant Black Hole. It emits no light, it reflects no light, and it absorbs any light that reaches it. It cannot be seen in our Universe.

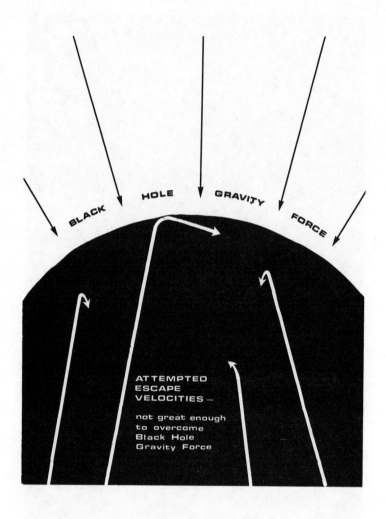

Figure 10. A representation of the enormously strong gravity field of a Black Hole. No velocity is high enough to escape and all matter and energy remain captured.

of light. But at this point we are up against another dimension — a fifth one, and this is mass-like. Again, the proper multiplier allows us to treat it mathematically, like a distance. It is a dimension into which we can travel in one direction but can't come out again. This is similar to the nature of time.

If we expand the size of our Black Hole so that it contains all the matter and all the energy in our Universe (a Super Black Hole), we now have an invisible holder into which our entire Universe can be tightly packed. It is conceivable that our Universe was in such a state before the Big Bang started it.

But science has a big problem. It hasn't yet figured out how to convert a Super Black Hole into a Big Bang.

Now that we are somewhat familiar with the concept of a Black Hole we can use this as a common starting point to explain certain relationships between science and the Bible (as there is nothing in the Bible which should prohibit this concept from being used). This is where we start the next chapter.

Chapter 8

THE BIBLE, TRUTH OR ALLEGORY?

Now that we have examined the two versions of the Earth's and man's history, let us see if it is possible to make them fit together. By way of review, science talks about a "Big Bang" as the start of our Universe some ten to twenty billion years ago. Our Galaxy formed some time afterwards. Our sun and its solar system are approximately five billion years old, which is also the age of the Earth and the Moon. Life on the Earth started over one billion years ago and originated in the ocean. Later, fish developed, then fowl, and finally, land animals. Man, the most highly developed land animal, is at least one million years old, and has been uncivilized for most of this time. Civilized man appeared suddenly about 6,000 years ago. Evidence of this civilization includes such activities as metallurgy, domesticating animals and developing the arts.

This 6,000 year figure becomes a crucial number in tying together science and the Book of Genesis. Notice its closeness to the Hebrew calendar which presently is slightly more than 5730 years old. 5735 in 1975 is the count of the years since the start of the Book of Genesis.

From the Book of Genesis we found that the creation of the world took place in seven "days." The first day started with nothing and ended after the creation of light. The second day is concerned with a firmament, or division, between waters. On the third day, dry land

TABLE 5.

COMPARISON BETWEEN EVENTS IN THE BOOK OF GENESIS AND SCIENCE

Science	Book Of Genesis
1. 10-20 billion years ago	Day 1. Light created.
2. Big Bang	Day 2. Firmament or separation of waters.
3. Shortly after Big Bang— formation of our Galaxy.	Day 3. Dry land appears; plant life.
4. 5 billion years ago — our solar system formed including sun, Moon, Earth.	Day 4. Sun and Moon created. Length of Earth day set.
5. One billion years ago — life started in oceans. Ultimately fish and fowl developed.	Day 5. Animal life started in oceans, followed by fish and fowl.
6. Land animals developed. About 1 million years ago mankind appears.	Day 6. Land animals, including man.
About 6,000 years ago — start of civilized man.	5730+ years ago — start of history of the Book of Genesis family.

appeared and the plant kingdom was created. The sun and the Moon were created on the fourth day, and the length of the day on Earth was also set. On the fifth day, animal life began in the ocean, and, on the sixth day, land animals were created, the last one being man. On the seventh day, God rested. Table 5 compares these two sets of data.

There appears to be general agreement between the events in the two columns in Table 5. *In fact, they could be describing the same events.* The major difference is in the time span. The key to this time problem can be found in the fourth day of the Book of Genesis when the creation of the sun and Moon set the time span of days on the Earth. Since these Earth days were never claimed to be the same length as the days of Creation, the use of "day" in the Book of Genesis can be considered as indicating an unspecified span of time rather than the time span in a 24 hour Earth day. This is a widely accepted biblical interpretation of the word "day" in "day of creation." With this in mind, the two columns appear to be even more closely related.

The Book of Genesis contains specific details about a set of families whose history began over 5700 years ago (chapter 3). Table 6 lists some of the more interesting characteristics and facts about this set of families.

Now we will attempt to fit the two columns in Table 5 together and try to explain the unusual facts in Table 6. To facilitate matters, we will use a method from the twelfth century Jewish scholar Maimonides who showed in his *Guide For The Perplexed*[3] that the substitution of a related word can sometimes clarify a

TABLE 6.

CHARACTERISTICS OF FAMILIES IN THE BOOK OF GENESIS

1. Live very long lives — over 900 years except for Enoch (365 years on Earth).

2. Bodies do not decay at death until the generation after Seth.

3. Can communicate with God.

4. Originally lived in the Garden of Eden which supported life for two people; tree of knowledge at center. Original pair forced to leave the Garden of Eden and live on Earth.

5. Introduced high civilization, including metallurgy, music, and animal husbandry.

6. All of Adam's surviving descendants, except Noah, died in the flood.

7. Life span falls during the 11th to 20th generation from over 900 years to 175 years (Abraham).

8. Males were marked (circumcized) from 20th generation onwards.

9. Aging of the body did not occur before Abraham.

10. Lingering death started after Isaac.

vague section of the Bible. We will substitute several precise, modern, technical but equivalent words for several words used in the Book of Genesis.

For a common starting point, we will make use of the Black Hole concept, discussed earlier (Chapter 7), in which a Black Hole was described as a massive gravity trap. Its gravity is so strong that it can capture nearby bodies, and nothing can escape from it, not even light. A Super Black Hole that could hold all the matter in our Universe is a conceptual possibility. It is a container in which the entire Universe can be stored. Since nothing escapes, there is no communication with our three-dimensional world. The "Black Hole" doesn't exist in our Universe. It is as though it were in another dimension — a dimension of mass or gravity. Since there is nothing in our Universe, it is empty or void and there is no light.

Up to the present time, science has not found a way to get matter out of the Super Black Hole, but the Book of Genesis states: ". . . the Earth was unformed and void [the Earth did not exist] and darkness was on the face of the deep." The term "deep" is usually thought of as a bottomless abyss, and a "black hole" is an acceptable modern substitute for "deep." "And the Spirit of the Lord hovered over the face of the waters." In twentieth century scientific terms, "face of the waters" could be translated as "surface of the fluids." Since the matter in a Black Hole is a fluid - a nuclear fluid rather than waters - a modern meaning of "face of the waters" is "surface of the Super Black Hole." The entire passage reads, "the Earth was unformed and void and darkness was on the surface of the Super Black Hole. And the Spirit of the Lord hovered over the surface of the Super Black Hole."

God said, "Let there be light," and the light appears. Certainly if anything starts to come out of a Black Hole, Science claims that the first thing to come out would be that which travels fastest — light. Thus, with the substitution of equivalent terms the Book of Genesis and science can be shown to agree that light is created first.

The Book of Genesis then says that a firmament separates or divides the "waters from the waters," or in modern technical terms, separates the "fluids from the fluids." So the fluids are forced apart by the firmament. This could be science's "Big Bang" of 10 or 20 billion years ago. Coincidentally, two types of fluids are mentioned in the Book of Genesis - fluids above and fluids below - and they are kept apart by the firmament. The terms "above" and "below" indicate that these fluids are opposite in nature, and science could perhaps identify matter fluids and anti-matter fluids as being the two "waters." Matter fluids and anti-matter fluids could both be expected to come out of a Super Black Hole. These fluids tend to attract each other and must be forced apart if they are not to collapse back into the Super Black Hole. The Book of Genesis also identifies Heaven as the firmament; thus Heaven is all of the space in which the Universe exists.

Next, the Book of Genesis says dry land appears. Science says solid land condensed from hot fluid matter. Thus both agree that the next step was the formation of the first worlds. However, science does not claim that our Earth was one of the first worlds.

The Book of Genesis states that the first life on these worlds was the plant kingdom. Science agrees that plant life developed first. Since plants require sunlight, and since our sun had not yet been created, there had to be other suns before ours!

The Book of Genesis states that when the sun and moon were created, the length of the day on the Earth was set. Science claims the sun, Moon and our own Earth were created about 5 billion years ago, after which the length of our day was set. The Book of Genesis continues with life in the sea, created in many forms, and this was followed by fowl. Science also says that animal life started on our Earth in the sea over one billion years ago, and developed into many forms, followed by fowl. The Book of Genesis and science both say that land animals were subsequently created, and that man was the last and most sophisticated land animal. Science says that Stone Age man is at least one million years old.

Thus we see that by starting from the Super Black Hole concept, there is agreement between science and the Book of Genesis. *They both could be describing the same set of events.*

Now let us account for the appearance of the Book of Genesis family some 5,700 years ago. From items 1, 2, 3 and 5 in Table 6, a modern mind would have to consider Adam and Eve as a pair of very superior beings. How do we fit this super couple into the archaeological record some 5,700 years ago, at just about the time archaeology says that Stone Age man achieved high civilization almost overnight? This superior couple lived in a "Garden" that had complete life support systems for the two of them. (The equivalent modern Persian word means enclosure rather than Garden). The "tree of knowledge at the center" could, in modern language, be translated as being a central computer, since knowledge is the important concept rather than the tree. What do we have today that provides life support for two people and is controlled by a computer? A twentieth century mind would immediately say a space ship.

Here I make the one major assumption of my concept — and that is, the Garden of Eden was a space ship that crash landed on the Earth, and that it carried two superior space people, Adam and Eve. We can find supportive evidence for it in the *Legends*, specifically the section on the Inhabitants of the Seven Earths. There we are told that there are six other Earths, that Adam visited the first two Earths, and that he bypassed the next four on his way to our Earth. The section which describes the Seven Earths is particularly interesting: "When Adam was cast out of Paradise, he first reached the lower of the Seven Earths" [the word "Earth" is used to describe all of these worlds] . . . . "it is dark, without a ray of light and utterly void." If we think of this as applicable to our own solar system, the terms lowest Earth and dark tend to make us think of the furthest known planet from the sun, Pluto (figure 3).

"On the second Earth, light is reflected from its own

sky . . . the ground bears neither wheat or any other of the seven species." Again, referring to our solar system, the second furthest planet is Neptune. This planet is large enough to have an atmosphere and thus a sky, and is undoubtedly too cold for wheat to grow. "The third Earth receives some light from the sun . . . there is neither wheat nor any other of the seven species," implying that the later planets are getting closer to the sun. The next closest planet in our solar system is Uranus which could get some light from the sun but is again too cold to grow wheat. "The fourth and fifth Earths, also do not have wheat." These Earths would correspond to Saturn and Jupiter in our solar system but, again, both probably are too cold for wheat. "The sixth Earth lacks water." This would correspond to Mars and the recent Mars flights have, indeed, shown that Mars lacks water on its surface. "The seventh Earth is the Earth inhabited by men." *This corresponds to our planet, Earth.* Figure 3 shows that the Earth is the seventh planet as we approach the sun. Is it merely a coincidence that a legend thousands of years old speaks of seven Earths, and that astronomically our Earth is the seventh planet as we approach the sun? It must be remembered that the ancients who wrote the material found in the *Legends* did not have telescopes and could not have known about the three farthest planets, Uranus, Neptune and Pluto.

For some reason, the space ship carrying our two space people crash landed on the Earth, because Adam and Eve had to leave it and live on the Earth among the Stone Age inhabitants. The Book of Genesis clearly states that Adam and Eve had to leave the Garden of Eden and live on the Earth. Adam and Eve must have been superior space men by comparison with the uncivilized Stone Age people who inhabited the Earth at the time. Their extremely long lives and non-decaying bodies are extraordinary evidence that there were some major differences.

But a real space man should have some remarkable gadgets, such as the shamir, the cutting tool which reportedly could cut diamonds, and which Solomon used in building the Temple. The *Legends* refer to a God-made suit of clothes, worn by Noah's grandson Nimrod, which made the wearer invincible and irresistible. The Sword of Methusaleh was supposedly used by Abraham when his small band of men conquered the armies of the five kings. Finally, the space ship itself carried a tree of knowledge and a tree of life. These are true space man devices!

Inasmuch as Cain and Seth are direct offspring of Adam and Eve, they, likewise, are space men. But where are wives to be found for them? There are Stone Age Earth females around, and Genesis (6:2) says: "The Sons of God found the Daughters of Man comely and took them for wives." In other words, space man *crossbred* with the indigenous population. Now the bodies of Seth's children decayed after death because they are only half space man, but they are still long-lived. Adam and most of his first nine descendants all died when they were more than 900 years old. The Book of Genesis says of them, "and he died" - all except the sixth one, Enoch, the father of Methusaleh. In his 365th year, Enoch "walked with God and was not of the Earth" (Genesis 5:23 & 24). In the *Legends*, the final paragraph of the "Translation of Enoch" states, "To the right of Enoch sparkled flames of fire, to the left of him burnt torches of fire, and on all sides he was encircled by storm and whirlwind, hurricane and thundering."

This text is thousands of years old to be sure, yet it could well be read in one of today's newspapers as it obviously could be describing a rocket launch. Those who watched the space launchings at Cape Kennedy will immediately see the resemblance. Does this mean the rocket was repaired and that Enoch took off in it to bring a rescue mission? Is this why a careful record of lineage and descendants is kept in the Book of Genesis? Is this why some of Adam's descendants are awaiting a messenger from God? Is it coincidence that Noah waited 500 years before he had children, long enough for Enoch to have returned if he had lived his normal 900 year life span? Is this where the Messiah concept originates? Does it also mean that the rising of the dead at the Messiah's return may be reserved for those space men whose bodies did not decay at death?

The family described in the Book of Genesis continues to the tenth generation, to Noah. Because none of Adam's other descendants survived the flood, it was no longer possible to breed within the group. As a result, space man had to cross breed a second time with the short-lived indigenous Earth people. In one generation, the life span dropped to 600 years, in another to 450 years, later to about 200 years, and continued to drop until it was only 175 years at the 20th generation (Abraham). The partial space men breed at an earlier age in these later generations, probably because they knew that their life span was shorter (see Table 1). And still the family record was kept. Yet, by now, it was becoming difficult to distinguish space man's descendants from Earth's indigenous people. Therefore, it became necessary to mark Abraham's descendants so they could be recognized. This could be the original reason for the inclusion of circumcision in the covenant with Abraham. For God promised the Land of Canaan to Abraham's heirs, and it was necessary to be able to identify them.

The Book of Genesis is a primogeniture history. It carries on the line through the first born son as the heir. Although this history details the generations from Noah to Abraham, it must be remembered that Noah had other descendants too. For example, he had three sons, 20 grandsons and at least 36 great grandsons (Chronicles: 1). Some of these great grandsons are clearly listed as being the progenitors of various peoples. While many people are descended from Adam through Noah, the Bible concentrates on the history of one of these groups of people — the group who first entered into a covenant with God.

The *Legends* relate that Adam's descendants did not age as they grew older. Abraham was the first in the Book of Genesis family to do so. Here again is evidence for a degeneration of a superior being. Furthermore, death came quite suddenly to Adam's descendants up till the time of Isaac. Only after Isaac was mankind afflicted with lingering death. Table 7 lists some of the major events in the degeneration of space man to Earth man.

The Book of Genesis states that Adam and some of his descendants talked with God. Could this be one of space man's abilities that has gradually disappeared as space man cross bred? Abraham, in the 20th generation, talked to God, but the ability seems to decrease afterwards. Moses was able to talk with God generations later. The last vestiges of communication with God appear to be the ability of the prophets to foretell the future and to bring warnings from God. In fact, the word prophet means "spokesman for God."

Now let's try to evaluate this theory using several criteria. The first criterion involves the number of assumptions that were made. Clearly a theory with dozens of assumptions is probably not likely to stand the test of time. In this case only one major assumption was made, i.e., *that the Garden of Eden was a space ship.* Another criterion for the acceptability of a theory is the number of major questions that the theory answers — the more the better. The space ship assumption permits us to answer many diverse questions, such as the source of the wives for Seth and Cain, the long lives of Adam and his first nine descendants, the decreasing life span of his next ten descendants, the origin of the Messiah concept, a possible reason for circumcision, and a number of others. In summary, the theory that is proposed here shows how the Book of Genesis can be interpreted in conjunction with modern science.

TABLE 7.

DEGENERATION OF SPACE MAN TO EARTH MAN

Name	Generation Number	Factor
Adam	1	Space man arrives on Earth.
Enosh	3	Body decays at death.
Shem	11	Life span falls to 600 years.
Arpachshad	12	Life span falls to 400 years.
Peleg	15	Life span falls to 239 years.
Abraham	20	Life span falls to 175 years.
Abraham	20	First to age as he grew older.
Jacob	22	First to die a lingering death.

It is important to note that even space men did not know how one person should act toward his fellow man on this Earth. Consider the difficulties between Abel and Cain. Furthermore the wickedness of Adam's descendants only ended with the flood. Noah recognized the need for a set of rules by which man could live on Earth, and the seven Noachide laws (Epilogue) are a set of rules for space man's descendants. Later, the Ten Commandments were set up for man, to guide him to live with his brothers. The problem of living together is still with us today, and its solution contains the secret of survival of all mankind.

Chapter 9

LIFE BEYOND OUR EARTH

Is it possible for life to exist elsewhere in the Universe? Could this life be technically superior to ours? Could superior space men visit our planet? Let us examine the various possibilities.

We will only consider life as we know it on the Earth. That is, we will suppose that evolution has created elsewhere in the Universe the same spectrum of life forms which populate our planet.

The oldest forms of life on the Earth are at least one billion years old. If Earth life has been duplicated elsewhere on the same time scale, that elsewhere must orbit a sun that has lasted at least one billion years. This means that all of the very large stars are not suitable to nurture life since large stars burn out in millions of years and do not last long enough.

Another important characteristic is the temperature on the Earth. Life, as we understand it, probably couldn't develop if the Earth's average temperature were either one hundred degrees colder or one hundred degrees warmer, because this would create problems with water freezing and boiling. Therefore, the very small and cold stars probably do not have planets warm enough to support life.

Thus, we are left with average stars like our sun. It is estimated that there are at least one billion such stars (out of a total of 100 billion) in our Milky Way Galaxy.

But not all of these one billion stars would be suitable for life as we know it. Most stars occur in pairs or even triplets. A planet that rotated around two suns would probably traverse a very erratic path in the sky, that is, it would alternate unevenly between very close approaches to one star and very distant passages around the other. The large temperature differences and the erratic weather would not be conducive to a uniform seasonal life pattern which some life follows on the Earth.

We must also eliminate from consideration those stars which have no planets. While the number of planets per star is important, the next most critical factor is the chemical and physical nature of the planet itself. The size of a planet would determine its gravity and this would affect the physical development of living bodies. However, a wide range of gravities is permissable for the development of Earth-style life. Gravity would also determine if the planet had an atmosphere and what gases would be present. If the planet were too small, perhaps the same size as our Moon, it would not have an atmosphere. The chemical elements on the surface of the planet are also important, but again a wide range is permissable. Within the limits discussed above, we would find that our Earth is probably not very unique in the Universe. *There should be many planets in the Universe which could support life.*

There are various estimates of the number of planets in our Galaxy that can sustain life, but a reasonable number is about one million planets [4]. Using generally

TABLE 8.

EARTH TIME VERSUS SPACE SHIP TIME

Elapsed Time At Starting Point In Earth Years	Elapsed Time Aboard A Sophisticated Space Ship
10 years	5 years
100	9
1,000	13
10,000	18
100,000	22

accepted Galaxy dimensions, the average distance between such planets can be computed to be several hundred light years. What are the possibilities for travel over such long distances? Obviously a man with a 70 year life span would not be expected to travel a distance that light traverses in several hundred years, even if he travels at the speed of light. But Einstein's Theory of Relativity explains the fact that if a man travels at speeds close to that of light, then time slows down for him.

Table 8 compares the elapsed time aboard a sophisticated space ship with the elapsed time at the launch site for a space ship that speeds up for half the trip*

*The acceleration is equal to the acceleration of gravity on the Earth.

and decelerates for the last half of the trip [4]. Enormous distances can be covered in relatively short periods of elapsed time if the space ship travels at speeds close to that of the speed of light.

If a space ship did come to the Earth some 5,700 years ago, where did it come from? There are no direct answers in the Book of Genesis, but there are at least three possible clues which can be found elsewhere. These clues point to a small group of stars, the *Pleiades*, roughly forming a question mark and embedded in a hazy cloud of light. Telescopic studies have shown that there are actually several hundred stars in this group, with seven bright stars. The number of visible stars varies between five and seven, depending on your visual acuity. It is visible in the winter sky, in line with Orion's belt but higher in the sky (Figure 11). The *Pleiades* are about 450 light years from us, and this distance could be covered in a reasonable time by a rocket travelling at almost the speed of light.

One of the references which suggests the *Pleiades* is mentioned in Job (9:8 & 9) where it says that God made the *Pleiades*. The *Legends* also refers to the *Pleiades*. One interesting passage relates that, in order to cause the flood at the time of Noah, God removed one of the *Pleiades* and allowed the waters above to rain down on the Earth. Another reference concerns the legend of a maiden named Istehar, who was taught by an angel the magic way to travel to Heaven. When she arrived there, she was placed among the stars of the *Pleiades*. In all of these instances, God is closely linked in some way with the *Pleiades*. Perhaps Adam's space ship came from the

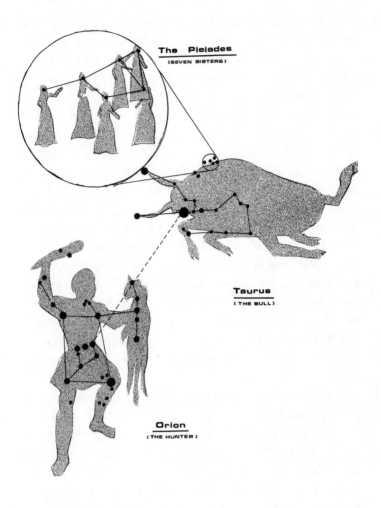

The Pleiades
(SEVEN SISTERS)

Taurus
(THE BULL)

Orion
(THE HUNTER)

Figure 11. Map of the northern night sky in winter show-
ing the location of the Pleiades. Only six of the seven
bright stars are shown, since most observers see only six
stars with the naked eye.

Pleiades. I am certain that there is other evidence that can be found in the Bible, if we knew how to look for it.

But if a rocket did crash land on the Earth and two space people settled on the Earth, how accurately would the story of this event be preserved? Let us look at a similar experience of a North American Indian tribe. This tribe, the Tlingit, lived on the northeast coast of Canada. Their first contact with European civilization was with the French navigator La Perause in 1786. The Tlingit had no written records and the story of the visit of La Perause was passed on by word of mouth. One hundred years later, a verbal report of the encounter was related by a Tlingit chief. The basic story was retained, but it also had acquired some mythological elements, especially for those things that the Tlingit did not understand. The French sailing vessels were described as immense black birds with white wings. Obviously the Tlingit's understanding was limited by their experience. The same problem existed for the Biblical observers.

If a space ship landed on the Earth and only an oral record was kept, we might expect that some of the major details would remain, but that changes would be made. These changes would fit the understanding of the story teller. As near as we can tell, the Book of Genesis recorded an oral tradition that was almost three thousand years old, and some changes were to be expected.

Is there other evidence that the Earth may have been visited by space people? E. Von Daniken [6] has made this his life long quest. He has found a number of unexplained things in various parts of the world that strongly suggest that there is evidence of space visitors. He asks provocative questions, but has never been able to authenticate to most scientists and critics, that we have had visitors from space. He raises questions about various sections of the Bible, for example Ezekiel, but does not propose that Adam and Eve were space travelers.

At this point, the entire subject of U.F.O.'s (unidentified flying objects) should be considered. Although about 90% of the sightings can be explained, there remain a small number of sightings which have never been satisfactorily explained. Are these U.F.O.'s really space vehicles that are controlled by extraplanetary intelligence? Some Earth people maintain that they have had contact with visitors from outer space. Certainly some of these accounts may not be entirely factual, and others may have been imagined. But let us suppose that even one of the more publicized events is true and the Earth has received interplanetary visitors within the recent past. This visit has had an almost negligible impact on our World and on our society. Very few people even believe that it happened. It is probable that the arrival of a space ship on Earth almost 6,000 years ago would not have had an immediate impact on the Stone Age society that existed here at the time. However, if a record were left, some of the important results would have come down to us. I have attempted to identify and to explain such records that are found in the Book of Genesis.

A technical assessment of the possibility of life

elsewhere in the Universe has been made by Carl Sagan and I. S. Shklovskii, in a book entitled "Intelligent Life in the Universe"[4]. Although some sections of this book are quite technical, it is very stimulating. The authors do not rule out the possibility of other life in the Universe and the possibility of communication and travel between civilizations. In fact, they make the statement that there may be as many as 50,000 planets that could sustain life.

Chapter 10

VISITORS FROM OTHER WORLDS

If a space ship from a very advanced civilization were to visit the Earth, what possible reasons could there be for the trip? Let us examine history and possibly find reasons for previous explorations and visitations on our Earth.

Exploration: Exploration of our solar system and our Earth by an advanced civilization is a distinct possibility. We ourselves have made a start in our own solar system by sending manned exploration expeditions to the Moon, by sending unmanned exploration ships to the nearby planets Venus and Mars, and by sending probe ships to the far away planets Mercury, Jupiter and Saturn. In addition to the possible military reasons, the purpose of our explorations is to learn about other planets, their resources, their life forms if any, and the existence and state of development of any civilization.

The rationale for contacting a newly discovered civilization would probably depend on the ultimate objective of the explorers. They may wish to keep their presence secret if the new-found civilization is hostile, or if it is so underdeveloped that meaningful and advantageous contact is futile, or if the explorers' future plans require secrecy. They may be willing to risk minimal contact if there were no hazard to themselves or if they wanted to interview or examine a few specimens of the existing civilization. The space travellers would have to protect themselves against any hostile acts while conducting an information exchange.

Missionary Work: There have been many missionary voyages through recorded history. By looking at history and the Bible, it is reasonable to suppose that a space mission could be bringing a message from God.

Colonization: A space ship could bring a small party of beings to colonize a planet. This could include cross-breeding with the existing inhabitants. If Adam and Eve did come to the Earth in a space ship, then colonization was indeed a possible reason since their descendants now fill our world.

Conquest: The conquest of one civilized world by another civilization could be another reason for space voyages. It is interesting that many interplanetary science fiction stories have conquest as a theme and that some science fiction stories have been very prophetic.

Refuge: People have left their homes to escape persecution, jail sentences and even death. This could be a good reason for a space voyage. There is a discussion in the *Legends* of fallen angels who rebelled against God and were expelled from Heaven. These beings could be seeking a life-supporting refuge somewhere in the Universe.

Wealth: Many expeditions in the past were motivated by a quest for riches. It is conceivable that an old civilization that has expended the resources on its own planet might be seeking new sources of supply on other planets. The economic costs of transporting these materials become important, but price is no object in obtaining necessities.

An Unknown Reason: A very advanced civilization may have reasons for a space voyage that we cannot understand or even imagine.

If an advanced civilization were considering a colonization expedition to a new planet, it would be very concerned about temperature and weather conditions. Climatologists have studied the Earth's weather and they believe that 3,000 to 6,000 years ago the Earth reached an optimum temperature regime for supporting life as we know it. Is it merely coincidence that the Garden of Eden existed some 5,700 years ago, just when the Earth's temperature turned ideal for colonization?

By examining the above lists of reasons for a space voyage, it becomes apparent that in many cases, one space voyage may not be enough. A series of voyages may, indeed, be needed. If Adam and Eve came to Earth in a space ship, it is possible that we have had other space ship visitors! There are other statements in the Bible that can be interpreted as space ships visiting Adam's descendants. For example, we are told that

Abraham was visited several times by angels from God. The angels visited Abraham on their way to destroy Sodom and Gemorrah (Genesis 18:2) and when he was about to sacrifice Isaac (Genesis 22:11). How did they travel to the Earth? Abraham was stopped from sacrificing his son to God when an angel called to him from out of Heaven. Was the angel in a hovering space ship?

There are several other incidents in the Bible which can readily be interpreted in terms of a space ship. Because men in biblical times did not understand a space ship, their descriptions would be obscure to us and expressed in terms that they knew. Let us interpret their words in a modern context.

A most amazing incident was described in the Book of Exodus (see reference 7). When the Israelites were wandering through the desert of Sinai, the Bible clearly states (Exodus 13:21 and 22) "And the Lord went before them by day in a pillar of cloud, to lead them the way and by night in a pillar of fire, to give them light, that they might go by day and by night: the pillar of cloud by day, and the pillar of fire by night, departed not from before the people." The pillar of cloud and fire was with the Israelites during the entire 40 years they spent in the Sinai desert. It also was apparently involved in the crossing of the Red Sea and the defeat of Pharoah's army: in Exodus (14:14), "The Lord will fight for you."; in Exodus (14:19 and 20), "And the pillar of cloud removed from before them, and stood behind them; and it came between the camp of Egypt and the camp of Israel."; in Exodus (14:24), "That the Lord looked forth upon the host of the Egyptians through the pillar of fire and of cloud." An angel moved with the pillar of cloud (Exodus 14:19) — "And the angel of God, who went before the camp of Israel, removed and went behind them; and the pillar of cloud removed from before them and stood behind them." God apparently uses the cloud, in Exodus (19:9): "And the Lord said unto Moses, 'Lo, I come unto thee in a thick cloud, that the people may hear when I speak with thee.'"

The pillar of cloud and light is involved in most of the crucial events that occurred in Sinai at that time. Could it in fact have been a space ship that was hidden in a cloud by day and was a glowing or fiery cylinder at night?

If a powerful sophisticated space ship were available to help the Israelites, then many of the miracles in the Book of Exodus could have been caused by such a vehicle. These include the manna in the desert, the fall of the walls of Jerico, the water flowing from rocks, the division of the Red Sea, the drowning of the Egyptian army, and the issuing of the Ten Commandments on Mount Sinai. One also wonders if the plagues that God loosed on the Egyptians were also accomplished from a space ship. These wonders include river water turning to blood, frogs leaving the river and over-running the land, gnats, flies, murrain (a disease of cattle), boils, hail, locusts, three days of darkness and slaying of the first born. Let your imagination wander and ponder the possible means by which these plagues could have been controlled from a space ship!

It is interesting that in Joshua (3:16) the Israelites crossed the Jordan on dry land. The waters of the

Jordan "stood and rose in a heap far off." The same phenomenon that occurred at the Red Sea was repeated at the Jordan! Some enormous power could stop the flow of a river as well as open a dry path through the sea. This capability can be understood in terms of a powerful space ship with its sophisticated equipment, and the extra-terrestrial abilities of its occupants.

There are also several incidents in the Book of Ezekiel that can be understood in terms of a space ship. One very detailed description can be found in reference 8. Ezekiel had four encounters with "The Hand of God" (Ezekiel 1:3, 3:22, 8:1, 40:1). The first encounter is the most descriptive. It speaks of a stormy wind, a great cloud with brightness, and fire flashing forth continually (1:4). This description of what we can interpret as a space ship is strange when we first read it, but we must remember that Ezekiel was apparently describing a space vehicle without ever having seen one or even knowing what it is. He can only use ideas and terms with which he was familiar, and so we must interpret his words with a twentieth century mind. One passage (Ezekiel 1) can be interpreted as a large space ship with four helicopter rotors suspended below it to provide maneuverability in the Earth's atmosphere. In fact, Ezekiel even went for a ride in the space ship for Ezekiel (3:12) says, "Then the spirit lifted me up, and as the glory of the Lord arose from its place, I heard behind me the sound of a great earthquake."

There is an incident in the second Book of Kings (2:11) where Elisha witnessed Elijah's ascent into Heaven. "And it came to pass . . . behold, there appeared a chariot of fire, and horses of fire, which parted them both asunder; and Elijah went up by a whirlwind into heaven." Clearly this can be visualized as a powerful flying machine, with fire coming from it, which picked up Elijah. It's interesting that just before this (II Kings 2:7) Elijah divided the waters of the Jordan and he and Elisha crossed over on dry ground. This feat may have been accomplished twice before by an earlier space ship. Once again there is the problem of Elisha describing an unknown device in terms that he knew, and once again a space ship is a good explanation in modern terminology.

There are other obscure passages in the Bible where the limited understanding of the observer resulted in a distorted description that is not immediately understood by a modern sophisticated reader. Reinterpretation of other such passages may uncover more evidence of space ship activities.

Now that we can see how the space ship concept serves to explain several sections of the Bible, can it be used to explain other more perplexing passages? For example, can a space ship which made a night landing with flaming, braking rockets appear as a bright star that crossed the night skies? Could this be the explanation for the Star of Bethlehem? Furthermore, the presence of a space ship could help explain many of the miracles in the New Testament, including even a Resurrection.

Chapter 11

PREDICTIONS

Every good theory should predict something new. If these predictions can be verified, they add credence to the theory. Can we make some predictions based on the theory that two superior space people cross bred with indigenous Stone Age people on Earth some 5,700 years ago? The following predictions are divided into two groups, the first of which deals with the consequences of the landing of an advanced space ship on Earth, and the second with future implications of such a landing for mankind.

Consequences of a Space Ship Landing on Earth 5,700 Years Ago

1. If there was a landing and takeoff of an advanced space ship some 6,000 years ago, it should be possible to find the landing site. Based upon the statement in Genesis (2:10) it should be near the headwaters of four rivers, two of which are the Tigris and the Euphrates, probably somewhere in the highlands of ancient Mesopotamia in the modern day countries of Iraq and Turkey.

2. If Adam and his direct descendants had bodies that did not decay, it should be possible to find the burial cave site in which the undecayed bodies of the original space man family still exist. (This assumes that a rescue mission has not removed them). The Bible claims the location of the burial Cave of Machpelah is

near Hebron on the west bank of the Jordan River. In fact, tourists today are shown a Cave of Machpelah and are told that Adam and Eve are buried in the lowest level. Were some special artifacts buried with them? Have the bodies decayed?

3. Since space man had some amazing superior instruments, ancient literature should be searched for mention of other space man devices. Perhaps these will be clues to finding the devices. In addition, some ancient literature may contain advanced technical ideas and concepts. However, translation may be impossible if the passage is not recognized as being a scientific treatise. There may also be some references to ancient "space men." A possibility exists that space men left a library of books that has become lost with time. For example, two of Noah's descendants, Shem and Eber, ran a school which Isaac attended. This school could have been a repository for a library filled with undreamed of knowledge. Can we find the site of this school?

4. There should be additional evidence for the abrupt rise of advanced civilization some 6,000 years ago. This should yield additional clues to space man.

5. If space man could communicate with God, there could be a remnant capability in his descendants on Earth today. Furthermore, there should be traces of other space man capabilities in some people on our Earth.

6. A rescue mission may have already arrived on the Earth. If a space ship was used for transportation, the landing and takeoff might have been spectacular.

Perhaps ancient literature contains references to this. We should consider the possibility that the rescuers may have tried to avoid contact with Man. There is also the possibility that a mission may come in the future!

7. Since the Bible claims that the Garden of Eden had many types of trees and plants, we should seek evidence of new botanical species that started in the Middle East about 6,000 years ago. Even as these words were written, scientists have just discovered that the cultivation of fruit (olives and grapes) started in the Middle East about 6,000 years ago [9].

8. When the skies are searched for signals from extraterrestrial civilizations, search carefully in the *Pleiades*.

Future Implications For Man

1. Today there are wide differences in human capabilities, intelligence, strength, etc. Could this partly be the result of an ancient cross breeding, or the lack of it, in the case of long isolated cultures? Can we try to undo the cross breeding to improve man and search for original space man characteristics? Are psychic powers just a remnant of some special capability of space man?

2. Can some of the other Biblical predictions be reinterpreted in light of this theory?

In order to investigate some of these predictions, exploratory efforts in the Middle East should be broadened. Suitable exploratory sites may be located by using old legends and literature and by surveying with modern instrumentation (e.g., magnetometer, scintillation counter). Excavations should also concentrate on finding a library of advanced information. The caves at Qumran took us back 2,000 years. Perhaps there is a cave that will take us back 5,000 years. There are probably important clues at the Cave of Machpelah.

Additional effort should be expended in a search among the inhabitants of our World for people with even slight concentrations of supernatural powers (for instance, with the ability to communicate with God). Finding authentic individuals may be very difficult because there will be an overabundance of fraudulent claimants. However, the discovery and development of persons possessing these powers may be helpful for the future of mankind.

Chapter 12

ANSWERS TO READER'S QUESTIONS

While reading this book, some questions will undoubtedly have occurred to the reader. This chapter contains questions and answers about the concepts presented in this book, and are typical of those which have been raised by various audiences which have heard this theory presented in lecture form. The questions are grouped into five main areas.

I. *Before The Arrival Of The Space Ship*

Q. The *Legends* claim that the light created on the first day could be seen from one end of Heaven to the other. Is there any explanation for this?

A. Using the Black Hole concept, the light of the first day could only travel a relatively short distance (one light day), and thus it is conceivable that it was possible to see from one end of the one day old Heaven to the other on the first day of Creation.

Q. The plant kingdom was created on the third day. But since plants require sunlight to live, and since our sun wasn't created until the fourth day, how and where did the plants get sunlight?

A. Other suns had to be created, or were in existence, before ours. In fact, dry land was created on the third day and this possibly was a world that revolved around some sun older than ours.

Q. What significance is there to the fact that Creation occurred in six days?

A. I do not know why the Book of Genesis divides Creation into six days. As explained in Chapter 8, the use of the term "day" is symbolic, since on the fourth day of Creation the length of the Earth's day was set. There is no statement or requirement that the Earth's day be of the same duration as a day of Creation. However, it is clearly obvious that God intended man to have one day of rest. Before the arrival of the space ship, indigenous Earth man was uncivilized and had to work seven days a week to hunt, to gather food, to find fuel and to defend himself. After Adam's descendants introduced some of the major facets of civilization, the division of labor and the growth of communities made it unnecessary for everyone to work every day. The Book of Genesis explicitly shows by God's example, that everyone should have a day of rest. In fact, the original conception of the Sabbath was a commemoration of Creation.

Q. Where did the space ship come from?

A. Since God "planted the Garden of Eden," he obviously made the space ship, and so the space ship came from God. The Book of Genesis states that Adam was 130 years old when Seth was born on Earth, and therefore, Adam's voyage to the Earth could not have taken more than 130 years. Even if his space ship could travel at the speed of light, we might suppose that the total distance Adam traveled could not have been more than the distance that light travels in 130 years time, or 130 light years. This selects a small volume of our Galaxy within which Adam could have started his trip. However, Einstein and relativity teach that when someone travels at the speed of light, time stands still for the traveler, so this approach does not identify all the possible starting points for the space ship. It was pointed out (Chapter 9) that between the Bible and the *Legends*, there are three references which link God to a group of several hundred stars called the Pleiades which is about 400 light years away from us. The Pleiades contains seven bright stars in the shape of a question mark; most of these bright stars are visible to the naked eye (see Figure 11). One reference in the *Legends* concerns an Earth girl Istehar, who was taught by an angel how to travel to Heaven. Her fate on arriving there was to be placed among the stars of the Pleiades. A second reference is found at the time of the flood; God removed one star from the Pleiades so that the waters above could flood upon the Earth. A third reference in Job (9:8 and 9) refers to "God who made the Pleiades."

Q. How long was the trip on the space ship?

A. Again there is no direct evidence, but because Seth was born on Earth when Adam was 130 years old, Adam's elapsed time for the trip had to be less than 130 years. Table 7 shows that the elapsed time aboard a sophisticated space ship could be quite short.

Q. What is the significance of the six other Earths before Adam came to our Earth?

A. From the descriptions of the other Earths, they are not capable of supporting life for Adam and his descendants. The final chosen planet, our Earth, can support life and happens to be the seventh planet when one starts counting from the outermost planet in our solar system. Is this only coincidence? The mathematical possibility of the ancient biblical writers guessing the correct number of planets is very low. This numerical piece of evidence, recorded thousands of years ago, agrees with the latest astronomical evidence obtained with modern telescopes.

Q. How do I associate a Tree of Knowledge with a computer?

A. The word "knowledge" is crucial in tying them together. The word "tree" may be symbolic or it may be a result of the limited understanding of those who first committed the Book of Genesis to writing. The tree of knowledge could just as easily be a knowledge device. As a point of interest, anyone who has ever looked at a diagram of a computer, will see a tree-like shape in the interconnecting cables.

Q. What was the forbidden fruit?

A. The fruit, or product of a computer, is an answer or a printout. To eat the fruit might mean to tamper with an answer or to destroy a printout. There could be many possibilities here.

II. *After The Arrival Of The Space Ship*

Q. Where did the space ship crash land?

A. The Book of Genesis makes reference to a confluence and headwaters of four rivers. One is the Tigris, one the Euphrates, and the two others use ancient names that are unknown today. The confluence might be in the mountains of Turkey where the two known rivers have their headwaters. If the repaired space ship did leave with Enoch, then the Garden of Eden is no longer on the Earth and that is why it has never been found.

Q. Is there any other evidence for the arrival and departure of a space ship?

A. Any physical evidence that existed was probably buried in mud during the flood, or was destroyed by the flow of armies across Mesopotamia (modern Iraq) in historical times. Perhaps there would be merit for some future archaeological expeditions to search for an ancient space ship landing site. This is a new approach since in the past the search was for a Garden of Eden. The evidence presented in this book mentions a cave that should contain the non-decayed bodies of the original space man family: Adam, Eve, Able and Seth. There is a cave at Hebron that is claimed to be the cave of Machpelah, the burial place of Adam's family. Perhaps careful examination of this and similar caves and their contents is warranted.

There might still be some evidence of Noah's Ark. There are recurring rumors of a ship-like structure frozen in the ice on Mount Ararat in Turkey. There is conjecture that this object could be Noah's Ark. But why is it so high up? Could an earthquake have raised the mountain in recent times?

Shem and Eber ran an academy to which Isaac was sent for instruction. Since this existed after the flood, there may be fantastic evidence buried at the site of this school.

Q. Is special significance attributed to the use of the word "Garden" if, in fact, it was a space ship?

A. The Book of Genesis says that the Garden of Eden had many types of plants and trees to provide food. When the space ship landed, we are told that Adam had to earn his bread from the Earth, that is, he planted a garden to grow food. This garden would be near the rocket ship. To the local Stone Age people, there would have been a visible garden; they could understand the Garden, but not the rocket ship. And perhaps that is why the Bible talks of a Garden of Eden.

Q. Who or what was the serpent?

A. The Book of Genesis describes the serpent as the closest to Man of all the animals of the field and that he walked upright on two legs. This could mean that he is a male from the Stone Age Earth people. If that were the case, he would have come aboard the space ship after it landed, and talked Eve into "eating the apple." The *Legends* claim that Cain was the offspring of Eve and the Serpent. The legendary Lilith* could have been Adam's Earth-born female. Was cross breeding by

Adam and Eve with Stone Age partners the original sin?

It should be noted that while the *Legends* mention the non-decay of Adam's, Abel's and Seth's bodies, it makes no such reference to Cain. This would be the case if he were a cross breed. Curiously, the Book of Genesis (Genesis 5:31) says of Seth that "Adam begot a son in his own likeness, after his image." No such statement is made about his first son Cain.

Q. If a space ship arrived with an advanced form of life, wouldn't it be likely that cross breeding would be impossible? For instance, man cannot mate with monkeys.

A. If a rocket ship were to land here at random, the possibility for cross breeding would be very small. However if God selected the landing place, he would have matched the biologies so that cross breeding could occur. We know nothing about life elsewhere in the Universe and it may be that a "mankind" type of life is rather common.

Q. Where did Seth and Cain get wives?

A. The Book of Genesis clearly says (Genesis

---

*Lilith: In folklore, a demon in the form of a beautiful woman who was supposed to have been the first wife of Adam. This story is told by Eve's descendants.

6:2) "that the Sons of God married the Daughters of Man." The first offspring of the space people are males. However, there were many Stone Age females about, and there were many to choose from.

Q. Why was there so much intermarriage among the members of Adam's family?

A. Modern biology does not recommend intermarriage between close relatives. Yet this was quite prevalent among Adam's descendants. If there was an effort to prevent the degeneration of a superior space man, the best way to try to preserve space man was to intermarry within the group.

Q. How do you explain the long life span of Adam and his first nine descendants?

A. Adam was a superior space man, and as such, his normal life span was over 900 years. Even though there was cross breeding after Seth, the near-space men still had long life spans of over 900 years.

Q. Why didn't the bodies of Adam and his sons decay while the bodies of Seth's sons did?

A. Since Adam and Eve were space people, their bodies apparently did not decay at death. Seth and Abel are direct offsprings, and their bodies also did not decay at death. Because the theory requires that

Seth sired his children with a female from the indigenous Stone Age Earth people, his children were only half space men and their bodies did decay at death. It's interesting to note that there is a Jewish tradition that the bodies of righteous men do not decay (i.e. Adam, Abraham, Moses, David). Perhaps an occasional descendant of Adam inherited some unique space man characteristics.

Q. Why did the life span drop after Noah?

A. During the flood, all of Adam's remaining descendants were wiped out. Noah's descendants had to cross breed again with the remaining indigenous Earth people. After this cross breeding, there wasn't enough space man left in these descendants to permit a 900 year life span. Noah's son, Shem, only lived some 600 years, and so the cross breeding could have occurred with Noah. This is reasonable since he had children late in life (at age 500) and he considered his relatives immoral. After Shem, man's life span drops to some 400 years and this could again be the result of further cross breeding.

Q. Where did the Messiah concept originate?

A. If Enoch did take the space ship back to God, then a return flight could be expected. This messenger from God would be awaited by Enoch's descendants. This is logically the earliest mention of the Messiah concept. Other evidence that a return flight is expected is that a careful record of ancestry is kept. In addition, the males were all marked by circumcision after Abraham, so they could be identified.

Q. How long was Enoch's return trip?

A. We don't know. If the space ship was damaged, then it might not have been travelling at maximum speed on the return trip. If he were travelling close to the speed of light, then time would move slowly for him, but the trip could take many more of our years.

It's interesting to speculate why Noah waited 500 years to have children. None of Adam's other descendants waited this long. Was he waiting for Enoch's return and did he only have children after he was sure that Enoch had lived out his 900 year life span?

Q. Did Enoch reach God after leaving the Earth in a space ship?

A. We do not know. If he did, then a rescue mission might be expected. There are other passages in the Bible where a space ship could be involved. For instance, the presence of a space ship could have created the miracles in the desert for

Moses. It could also facilitate his talking
to God. And there is mention that the
Israelites in Sinai followed a cloud by day
and a bright light by night (Chapter 11).
The little known Book of Enoch[11] was lost
to western scholars for almost 2000 years.
Enoch tells of visiting Heaven and makes
predictions for the future. His trip to
Heaven can be interpreted as a space ship
voyage.

Q. How do you explain some of the remarkable gifts that God gave Adam, such as
the Shamir that cuts diamonds and a
marvelous suit of clothing that made
Nimrod a great hunter?

A. Aboard any modern space ship, there
would be many devices and materials
which would appear miraculous to uncivilized people. If some of these were
removed before Enoch left with the space
ship, they would be gifts from God to the
people left behind on Earth. In fact, a
space ship provides a simple answer for
the source of these devices.

Q. What is the significance of the Tower of
Babel?

A. The Tower of Babel concerns a dispersion
of language among the descendants of
Noah. It could also mean a dispersion of
people and thus a great deal of cross
breeding with the indigenous Earth

people. From this time on, cross breeding reaches all the people of the Earth and we are, indeed, all brothers. The Book of Genesis is a primogeniture history as it follows the first son or first heir only. The other offspring are not closely followed.

Q. The evolution of a Stone Age people on the Earth doesn't agree with the origin of man in the Bible. Is there any explanation for the difference?

A. The Bible is a history of the family of two space people, Adam and Eve. It does not concern itself with a Stone Age Earth people, even though they may have been used for cross breeding purposes.

Q. If Adam was a space man, why wasn't his superior knowledge handed down?

A. Since Adam lived to see seven generations of his descendants (Figure 1), it was unnecessary for them to learn all that he knew since he was available to answer questions. Furthermore, after the rocket left, there was even less need for advanced technical data. What was needed was information which would make life easier for his descendants. We know that some information was handed down about metallurgy, the arts, and animal husbandry. A moral code was also provided.

Furthermore, the flood wiped out almost

all of Adam's descendants except Noah who had probably learned a great deal from his elders. A very technically sophisticated man is critically dependent on his entire society for tools and materials. Look at the Robinson Crusoe story. Much of what he knew was almost useless to him because he lacked tools and materials. He had to start from scratch for everything. Imagine yourself on a deserted island. You must make everything for yourself since there is no source of finished materials. You would have to cut trees for lumber, find your food and water, provide material and make clothing and build your own shelter. There would be no readily available coal or oil for fuel and no electricity for power. You would even need to find iron ore to make iron, assuming you knew how to do it. The Robinson Crusoe story shows that even a very technically advanced person is severely limited when he is alone and isolated.

Q. Archaeology speaks of two sites as the source of high civilization: (1) somewhere along the Tigris-Euphrates, and (2) Egypt, along the Nile. How do you reconcile these two sites with this theory?

A. The Book of Genesis teaches that Cain left his parents and settled "east of

Eden." Thus, in fact, there should be two sites where civilization started, the first descended from Adam and Seth and the second from Cain.

III. *Long Range Implications Of This Theory*

Q. How did I remove the apparent conflict between science and the Book of Genesis?

A. I used modern technical words which were the equivalent of some of the general words in the Book of Genesis. This is similar to what Maimonides did in his *Guide For The Perplexed* where he substituted similar words in order to explain vague biblical passages. I maintain that the common words used in the Bible do not give the modern technical connotation, and thus prevent the similarities from being evident. They were the best words available to the compilers of the Bible. I use the events of the fourth day of Creation to show that an Earth day is different in length from a day of Creation. I use the Black Hole concept as a suitable starting point for the Book of Genesis and for science. The only fundamental assumption I make is that *the Garden of Eden was a space ship.*

Q. If there is no conflict between the Book of Genesis and science, where do they both lead?

A. Science can no longer say that the Genesis version of Creation is incorrect. Now Genesis can be accepted, by some people, on more than just faith. In addition, it is evident that *whoever wrote the Book of Genesis knew as much about the Creation of the Universe as modern science does and he knew about it several thousand years ago.*

Q. How does this theory lead to a reason for circumcision of Abraham's male descendants?

A. As the shortened life span of Adam's descendants started to approach that of the indigenous Stone Age people on the Earth, it was becoming increasingly difficult to distinguish Abraham's descendants from the rest of the world's people. Since they were awaiting a messenger from God and were to inherit the land of Canaan, it became necessary to mark them for future identification. Male circumcision just after birth is a very positive marking system, and it was passed on through future generations as a religious requirement of Judaism.

Q. Has a rescue mission come?

A. It is conceivable that Enoch reached God and returned[11], or the return trip may have been made by some other messenger. In either case, the messenger would be a space man. Perhaps the word "angel" might be more suitable. Any messenger probably would be more advanced than we, and would no doubt be cautious about revealing himself. What would his mission be? One mission might be to rescue or retrieve the non-decaying bodies of Adam and Eve to take them back to God. After all, Adam left specific instructions for his burial.

But what about the cross breeds left on Earth, that is, we the people of Earth? The Book of Genesis says the sins of the father shall be visited on the sons, and Adam was told he would earn his bread by the sweat of his brow. I interpret this to mean that we will remain on this planet Earth. Clearly, the Bible set down a code of conduct for us delineating man's responsibility to his fellow man. Part of the messenger's mission to us would undoubtedly involve man's relationship to his fellow man, for the arrival of the Messiah is supposed to usher in an age of peace.

Q. Could some of the U.F.O. sightings be messengers from God?

A. A small percentage of the U.F.O. events have not been explained. It is possible that there is a real space ship among these events. None of these U.F.O.'s have announced themselves as being messengers from God, nor have they been identified as being messengers from God.

IV. *Philosophical Questions*

Q. Do I believe this theory?

A. The important thing is not whether I believe this theory, but rather to realize that *with one assumption and by translating a few words into modern usage, one can obtain remarkable agreement between science and the Book of Genesis.* The conflict is removed. Perhaps there are other interpretations of the Book of Genesis and I encourage the reader to seek his own. A theory does not have to be right. It only has to explain a set of facts.

Q. How do you justify changing some of the words in the Book of Genesis?

A. Maimonides did a similar thing in his *Guide for the Perplexed*, where he substituted similar words in obscure passages in order to obtain clearer biblical meanings. I do not use words at random. I substitute a modern technical word for the general word, but the meanings are essentially unchanged. The technical words explain the text in modern scientific terms that clarify the meaning for a twentieth century reader. The compilers of the Book of Genesis did not have the scientific knowledge and terminology that we do.

Q. How would you summarize the way science and the Book of Genesis fit together?

A. The Book of Genesis tells us what happened and science tries to explain how it happened.

Q. If science can no longer be used to deny the technical aspects of the Book of Genesis, can science now agree with the revelation part of the Book of Genesis, specifically the existence of God?

A. Science has never denied the existence of God. Science is not qualified to judge about the existence of God since, I believe, that subject is out of its domain. In fact, science has learned that our World runs on a very logical and wonderful system. Since science can be shown to agree with the Bible, it can no longer be used to question the technical aspect of the Book of Genesis.

Q. Could there be life in other places in the Universe?

A. *Yes, I think it is conceivable that there is life elsewhere in the Universe* (see Reference 8). Science does not yet know enough to guess where it might be or what type of life it is. However, if space man did come to Earth in a space ship, then he had to originate some place. And since he was a space man, his civilization must be very advanced in comparison with ours.

Q. Is there a life after death?

A. If man's body dies, his memory must also die since memory is a chemical and electrical function in the brain. It is difficult to see how an eternal soul if one exists, could take with it the dead memory of the body it has left. The Book of Genesis (3:22) talks of a Tree of Life in the Garden of Eden, and if Adam were to eat of it he would become immortal. Equipped with a non-decaying body, it might be possible for space men to live forever under the proper conditions. Apparently these conditions could be met by eating of the Tree of Life. So immortality may be possible for space man if he gets the proper nourishment. Man's body is not the same as space man's and, therefore, man's body is not immortal.

Q. Why doesn't God intervene more frequently in human affairs with miracles?

A. God created an entire Universe that follows certain laws. The Universe runs itself. Man, as part of that Universe, must also follow a set of laws. But only man can make the free choice between good and evil. In either case, the laws of the Universe prevail. If man is collectively good, he can establish a Heaven on Earth. If he is collectively evil, he can create a hell.

There may be particular situations in which one might hope for divine intervention. But this hope arises from a human point of view. God's view may be completely different, one that we as human beings cannot even understand.

Q. What is God?

A. I do not know. Many people have found very personal answers. Perhaps we can make a small start on an answer by enumerating some characteristics. According to the Book of Genesis, God was able to remove our entire Universe from a Super Black Hole. Since then, the Universe has followed a systematic set of laws that were probably set in operation at the time of the "Big Bang." God existed before the Big Bang and may have existed for whatever time existed before that.

V. *Questions Directed To The Author*

Q. Why did you write this book?

A. I developed this concept to satisfy my scientific curiosity as to why science and the Book of Genesis did not agree. When my children were in college, I found that they also had the same questions and they found my answers very interesting. I extended my audience by lecturing to small groups and found that many people were intrigued by this theory. I was gratified that so many young students went back and voluntarily read the Bible after listening to this theory. Some of my audience suggested that I expand this material into a book so that I could reach a larger audience. This book is the result. Also, there was the intellectual challenge of writing a book and seeing it published.

Q. How did you become interested in this subject?

A. I received a religious education and studied the Bible for many years. My profession as a physicist required a very extensive scientific education. In fact, cosmology and cosmogony are hobbies of mine, and science's version of Creation is a very good one. For a long time it bothered me that there was a conflict between the words of science and the words of the Book of Genesis. Was there any way to remove the conflict? Under what conditions do they fit together? Could science and the Bible be talking about the same set of events? From this set of questions, I slowly developed my theory and answers.

Q. Isn't this theory similar to that of Von Daniken (Reference 6)?

A. Von Daniken only asks "speculative questions." He has not authenticated any answers. My concept was developed independently of Von Daniken. He does not claim Adam and Eve to be space men, and he doesn't claim that the Garden of Eden was a space ship. I work strictly from the Book of Genesis and other related materials and I attempt to justify my assumptions by utilizing these materials and by generating plausible answers to some very difficult biblical questions.

Q. Other authors also speak of superior space visitors to our planet. How do your ideas differ?

A. I work only within the framework of the Book of Genesis. My only assumption is that the Garden of Eden was a space ship and that Adam and Eve were space people. I know of no other author who has yet done this.

EPILOGUE

Beyond Now

There has always been agreement between the Bible and the social sciences with regard to morality. But now we can also find agreement between the Book of Genesis and physical science, and this puts all of the Bible on a firmer basis. The fundamental teaching of the Bible, that man must learn to live with other men, has even greater meaning.

It is interesting to trace some of the major events in this area. Even the spaceman Cain was originally unable to live with his siblings and other relations. A set of rules was needed so that spaceman could survive among, and with, his fellow man. God gave Adam and Noah a set of seven laws, the Noachide Laws, for this purpose. There are prohibitions against idolatry, blasphemy, murder, sexual immorality, theft and eating the flesh (limb) of a live animal. There was also a requirement to set up a rule of law (courts). But Noah's spaceman antecedents did not heed the laws and were wiped out in the flood. By Moses' time, the rules had been modified and extended into The Ten Commandments. These included prohibitions against idolatry, graven images, blasphemy, murder, adultery, stealing, bearing false witness and coveting, as well as positive requirements to honor parents and keep the Sabbath. But the same clear message keeps coming through — Do unto others as you would want to be done unto you.

111

And science, in its way, supports this lesson so that men will be better able to live with each other.

In this book I have presented a theory to explain the Book of Genesis in space age terms. Scientific agreement with the biblical account of Creation may not be necessary for many readers, because those who look to the Bible for comfort usually find peace of mind and heart without difficulty.

There are others, however, who constantly strive for new interpretation and understanding. Realizing that you may not accept all of the ideas I have presented, I offer you this challenge: Reexamine the Bible and find out for yourself how its teachings are relevant to your life today!

To you, the reader, who has the courage to continue the search for the ultimate meaning of life and for God . . . . I dedicate this book.

GLOSSARY OF TERMS

Abraham (Abram)

Name of Adam's nineteenth descendant in the Book of Genesis. God gave him the name Abraham after their covenant. Before that time his name was Abram. This name change is also believed to have occurred as a result of a language change from Aramaic to Hebrew.

Anti-matter

The matter contained in our Earth and Solar System has certain electrical properties (positive nucleus and negative electrons). Anti-matter has the opposite electrical nature (negative nucleus and positive electrons), but otherwise is identical to normal matter. When matter and anti-matter are brought into contact, they annihilate each other's mass and they are converted into an equivalent amount of energy.

Archaeology

The scientific study of material remains of past human life and activities.

Astronomy

The science of the celestial bodies and of their magnitudes, motions and constitution. It includes the Solar System, our Galaxy and the Universe.

Big Bang

The most accepted theory explaining the start of the Universe. The Big Bang was an enormous explosion which started the Universe expanding

113

out from its initial densely packed condition. Although this occurred between 10 and 20 billion years ago, the fragments of the Universe are still flying away from each other.

Black Hole

A massive gravity trap from which nothing can escape, not even light. Because no light escapes, it is black, and because matter falls into it, it is a "hole" in our Universe through which matter can leave our Universe but cannot return. We can envisage a "super" black hole (that which contains all the matter in the Universe) to be the container from which the Big Bang blew apart.

Cosmogony

The study of the origin of our Universe.

Cosmology

The study of the history and development of our Universe. It does not include a study of the start of the Universe which is the distinct science called cosmogony (see above).

Covenant

Agreement between God and Abraham wherein God promised the land of Canaan to Abraham's descendants and, in addition, he would be their God. They, in turn, were to have only the one God and the males were to be circumcised as a sign of the Covenant.

Day of Creation

There are a total of seven "days" during which the Universe and man were created. On the fourth Day of Creation, the Earth's day is identified separately from a Day of Creation. Therefore, a Day of Creation denotes a period of time. In this book, different lengths of time are assigned to each of the six Days of Creation to effect a fit between science and the Book of Genesis.

Earth

The third planet away from the sun in our solar system. It is about 8000 miles in diameter and is the only planet in our solar system which has a blue color. The color is due to the oceans reflecting the blue of the skies.

Earth Day

The time it takes our planet to spin once on its axis is called an Earth day. During this time, a point on the Earth's surface faces toward the sun for about half the day and is in the Earth's shadow for the other half of the day. In the Book of Genesis, the length of the Earth's day is set (fixed) on the fourth Day of Creation when the sun and Moon are created.

Escape Velocity

Because the gravity of an astronomical body attracts all things to that body, escape from the body becomes possible only when the velocity is high enough to overcome the pull of the gravity field. The more massive a body, the stronger the gravity field, and hence, the higher the escape velocity.

Evolution

Evolution is a theory which concerns the development of higher life forms on our planet. The first living animals were small single cells in the ocean.

Slowly their size increased through the combination of many cells and the development of special cells to perform specific functions. The development goes from single celled animals to fish to amphibian to reptile to mammal to primate to man. Charles Darwin was one of the early proponents of this concept.

Firmament

The vault, or expanse, of Heaven is the common meaning of firmament. The Book of Genesis claims that the firmament divided or separated the matter in existence on the second Day of Creation. As such, it is comparable to the scientific concept of the Big Bang which also separated (or forced apart) matter at the start of our Universe.

Galaxy

The Galaxy is the enormous family of stars of which our sun is an average member. Our Galaxy is disk-shaped with an expanding spiral in the disk. It is estimated that there are over 100 billion stars in our Galaxy.

Garden of Eden

The original home of Adam and Eve in the Book of Genesis is called the Garden of Eden. It provided everything needed to support life for the two occupants. At its center was a Tree of Knowledge of Good and Evil, and a Tree of Immortality. Adam and Eve were forbidden to eat of these trees.

Genesis

The first Book of the Old Testament. It starts with a discussion of the Creation of the World and ends with the death of Jacob's son Joseph in Egypt.

Geology

The science concerned with the study of the Earth.
It includes the classification and origin of various
rocks, the history of the Earth's surface features,
and the internal structure of the Earth.

Gravity

Since all matter attracts each other, the resultant
attractive force of all the matter in a planet is
called the gravity or gravitational field of the
planet.

Istehar

An Earth maiden who, according to the *Legends of
the Bible* was loved by an angel. She found out
from him how to ascend to Heaven and, when she
arrived there, she was placed among the stars of the
Pleiades.

Legends (or Legends of the Bible)

A one volume condensation of the six volume work
written by Rabbi Louis Ginzberg and published in
1972. It contains the so-called oral tradition of the
Bible. Much of the material was not included in the
Old Testament. However, some of it is available in
Jewish Commentaries on the Bible, (The Talmud),
writings of the Church fathers, and as oral tradition.

Matter

Matter is that which fills empty space. Science
teaches that two things resulted from the Big Bang:
(1) matter, and (2) energy. Einstein taught that
matter and energy are interchangeable. The Book

of Genesis also teaches that energy (as light) and matter (as water and dry land) were the first things created.

Messiah

The Bible contains a prophesy that a Messiah, or Messenger from God, will arrive on Earth and announce God's kingdom on Earth. The dead will rise and there will be an era of peace and brotherhood on Earth.

Metallurgy

The scientific study of a class of elements known as metals is called metallurgy. These elements are characterized as opaque, having a specific type of lustre, and generally being fusible and good conductors of heat and electricity.

Noachide Code

The Noachide Code is a group of seven laws given by God to Adam and Noah. They deal with the relationship between man and God and between man and man. There are prohibitions against idolatry, blasphemy, shedding blood, sin in sexual relations, theft, and eating the flesh of a live animal. There was also a requirement to set up a rule of law.

Pentateuch

The Hebrew name for the first five books of the Bible. These are Genesis, Exodus, Leviticus, Numbers, and Deuteronomy.

Planet

A solid body, usually almost spherical, that is under the gravitational control of a star. A planet

118

orbits around the star. Our Earth is the third planet in orbit around our sun. The time for one orbit is one planetary year.

Pleiades

A group of stars usually seen in winter. There are about seven visible stars, in the shape of a question mark, contained in a hazy patch of light. Telescopes show several hundred stars and their distance is computed as about 400 light years from the sun.

Qumran Caves

The Caves at Qumran are near the Dead Sea where 2,000 year old copies of the Old Testament were recently found. Modern texts and the Dead Sea scrolls show few discrepancies.

Science

The knowledge ascertained by observation and experiment, critically tested, systematized and brought under general principles is called science. Science's function is to explain nature.

Septuagint

The first Greek translation of the Bible. It was produced in Alexandria in about the second century B.C. The term derives from the fact that some 72 scholars worked on it, supposedly six from each of the 12 tribes.

Shamir

The shamir is a device, mentioned in the *Legends*, that could be used to cut stones and scratch diamonds. It supposedly was used by Solomon in building his Temple since no iron tools were permitted to be used in its construction. It disappeared after the Temple was built.

Sociology

The study of man and his relationships with others is called sociology. It includes studies of human cultures.

Solar System

A family of astronomical bodies consisting of a central star (or stars) and a set of orbiting bodies called planets. Other minor bodies such as comets may also be included. The central star controls the motion of the planets by its gravitational field. Our sun has nine planets in its solar system and ours is the third from the sun.

Talmud

Commentaries on the Bible that were written in the millenium after the Bible was completed.

Ten Commandments

A code of behavior for man given by God to Moses. It contains prohibitions against idolatry, graven images, blasphemy, murder, adultery, stealing, bearing false witness, and coveting. There are requirements for honoring parents and keeping the Sabbath.

Theology

The study of God, and his relation to the world.

Theory

An explanation of anything is called a theory if it is supported by facts. In science a theory usually starts with an assumption(s) and attempts to justify that assumption with facts and evidence.

Time Dilation

Relativity teaches that time span is not the same under all conditions. When speeds are very close to the speed of light, time becomes stretched out and passes more slowly for those traveling at such speeds.

Tree of Knowledge

There was a tree at the center of the Garden of Eden. Adam was instructed not to eat of this tree or he would die. Theologians say that this was a Tree of the Knowledge of Good and Evil and that by becoming aware of Good and Evil man had to choose between them.

Tree of Life

The Tree of Life was another tree in the Garden of Eden. Man was not to eat of this tree lest he became immortal.

Universe

The Universe is the entire existing physical system in which we live. Its major components are Galaxies which are rushing away from each other. The Universe is some ten to twenty billion years old. Science says it started with a Big Bang and the Book of Genesis says it started with light, followed by waters forced apart by a firmament.

Year

Time needed for the Earth to circle once around the Sun. On another planet, it would be the time required for that planet to circle its sun.

REFERENCES

1) *Holy Scriptures* — The Masoretic Text — 1955. Jewish Publication Society of America, Philadelphia.

2) Ginzberg, L. (1972). *Legends of the Bible* (one volume edition). Jewish Publication Society of America, Philadelphia.

3) Maimonides, M. (1956 version). *The Guide For The Perplexed.* Dover, New York.

4) Sagan C. and Shklovskii, I. S. (1966). *Intelligent Life in the Universe.* Holden Day, San Francisco.

5) Keller, W. (1956). *The Bible as History.* Wm. Morran and Company, New York.

6) Von Daniken, E. (1970). *Chariots of the Gods.* G. F. Putnam Sons, New York.

7) Downing, B. H. *The Bible and Flying Saucers.* Avon.

8) Blumrich, J. F. *The Space Ships of Ezekiel.* Bantam, New York.

9) Zohary, D. and Spiegel, Ray, P. *Beginnings of Fruit Growing in the Old World.* Science: 187, 319; January 31, 1975.

10) Taylor, J. (1974). *Black Holes,* Random House, New York.

11) Charles, R. H. (1912). *Book of Enoch.* Oxford, London.